T0295567

**Advanced Introduction to Marketing Strategy**

**Elgar Advanced Introductions** are stimulating and thoughtful introductions to major fields in the social sciences, business and law, expertly written by the world's leading scholars. Designed to be accessible yet rigorous, they offer concise and lucid surveys of the substantive and policy issues associated with discrete subject areas.

The aims of the series are two-fold: to pinpoint essential principles of a particular field, and to offer insights that stimulate critical thinking. By distilling the vast and often technical corpus of information on the subject into a concise and meaningful form, the books serve as accessible introductions for undergraduate and graduate students coming to the subject for the first time. Importantly, they also develop well-informed, nuanced critiques of the field that will challenge and extend the understanding of advanced students, scholars and policy-makers.

For a full list of titles in the series please see the back of the book. Recent titles in the series include:

Family Policy
*Chiara Saraceno*

Law and Psychology
*Tom R. Tyler*

Advertising
*Patrick De Pelsmacker*

New Institutional Economics
*Claude Ménard and Mary M. Shirley*

The Sociology of Sport
*Eric Anderson and Rory Magrath*

The Sociology of Peace Processes
*John D. Brewer*

Social Protection
*James Midgley*

Corporate Finance
*James A. Brickley and Clifford W. Smith Jr*

U.S. Federal Securities Law
*Thomas Lee Hazen*

Cybersecurity Law
*David P. Fidler*

The Sociology of Work
*Amy S. Wharton*

Marketing Strategy
*George S. Day*

Advanced Introduction to

# Marketing Strategy

GEORGE S. DAY
*Geoffrey T. Boisi Emeritus Professor, The Wharton School, University of Pennsylvania, USA*

**Elgar Advanced Introductions**

 **Edward Elgar**
PUBLISHING

Cheltenham, UK • Northampton, MA, USA

Published by
Edward Elgar Publishing Limited
The Lypiatts
15 Lansdown Road
Cheltenham
Glos GL50 2JA
UK

Edward Elgar Publishing, Inc.
William Pratt House
9 Dewey Court
Northampton
Massachusetts 01060
USA

A catalogue record for this book
is available from the British Library

Library of Congress Control Number: 2022934684

Printed on elemental chlorine free (ECF)
recycled paper containing 30% Post-Consumer Waste

ISBN 978 1 80037 788 2 (cased)
ISBN 978 1 80037 790 5 (paperback)
ISBN 978 1 80037 789 9 (eBook)

Printed and bound in the USA

# Contents

# About the author

George S. Day is the Geoffrey T. Boisi Emeritus Professor in The Wharton School at the University of Pennsylvania, USA. He was previously the Executive Director of the Marketing Science Institute, and the Founder and Co-Director of the Mack Institute for Innovation Management.

He has been a consultant to corporations such as General Electric, IBM, Unilever, W.L. Gore, Boeing, LG Corp., Best Buy, Merck, Johnson & Johnson, Agilent and Medtronic. He is the past Chairman of the American Marketing Association. He has also served on ten boards of directors.

Dr. Day has authored nineteen books including *Strategy from the Outside-In: Profiting from Customer Value*, with Christine Moorman

(2010), *Innovation Prowess* (2013), and *See Sooner, Act Faster*, with Paul Schoemaker (2019).

He has won ten best article awards and one best book award. He was honored with the Parlin Award in 1994, the Converse Award in 1996, the Sheth Foundation award in 2003, the Mahajan Award in 2001 and the William L. Wilkie award in 2017. In 2003 he received the AMA/Irwin/ McGraw-Hill Distinguished Marketing Educator Award. In 2011 he was chosen as one of eleven "Legends in Marketing." In 2021 he received the Sheth Medal.

# Preface

> The purpose of a business is to create and keep customers at a profit.
> (Peter F. Drucker, 1954)

Welcome to this advanced introduction to marketing strategy. If you are reading this preface, you will be familiar with the essentials of marketing that are the foundations of a marketing perspective on strategy. These essentials include: the four Ps, STP (segmentation, targeting and positioning), the product life cycle, customer lifetime value and marketing metrics. You'll also know about the marketing concept, which holds that the purpose of a business is to profitably create and keep customers.

These staples of marketing are sound starting points for formulating a strategy, but offer limited guidance for dealing with the cross-cutting forces shaping the markets of the future. These forces include the digital transformation of all business activities, increasing global trade tensions, customer's rising expectations for a personalized and integrated experience, the emergence of powerful platforms and, perhaps, a new medium of exchange with crypto-currencies. Meanwhile the societal demands on businesses to respond to ESG (environmental, social, governance) issues are mounting. A next-generation marketing approach is needed to help businesses navigate and profit from mounting turbulence and the resulting uncertainty, and ensure the marketing function contributes fully to the strategy dialogue with deep insights and the capabilities needed to deliver marketing activities better than their rivals.

An advanced approach to marketing strategy starts from the outside in, by taking the point of view of key market stakeholders (customers, consumers, competitors and channel partners) to view the firm and its future prospects objectively. The aim is to find the best ways to offer *superior value to the customers the business chooses to serve*, and then innovating new customer value to stay ahead of rivals. These are the integrating themes of an advanced approach to marketing strategy, and answer the fundamental strategy questions of "where to play, and how to win." We'll situate this outside-in approach within the cognate fields of competitive strategy and design thinking, and presume some familiarity with strategy-making processes, activity systems, value chains, the structural analyses of industries, as well as the emerging stakeholder view of business.

Our vantage point on these strategic issues will be the leadership team or C-suite, in their roles as strategy advisers to the chief executive officer and the board of directors, with responsibility for executing the chosen strategy and meeting the performance objectives. Within this top team, the advocate for taking an outside-in approach should be the chief marketing officer whose credibility is derived from deep market insights and wide-ranging knowledge of the strategic moves that prepare the business for a more turbulent future.

The quote by Peter Drucker that starts this Preface has been a touchstone for marketers for almost 70 years, and we are still guided by his wisdom. Drucker did not see himself as a marketer; but because he saw marketing as a core responsibility of management his thinking continues to shape the field of marketing. He also said: "Marketing is so basic it cannot be considered a separate function within the business ... it is the whole business seen from the customer's point of view" (Drucker 1954). This is the essence of the outside-in approach to strategy.

This advanced introduction is another milestone in my career-long journey to develop and apply new ways of thinking about business strategy and the capabilities of organizations, to the daunting task of sustaining competitive advantages in a turbulent world. This journey began in 1977 when I diagnosed the flawed assumptions of the Boston Consulting Group (BCG) portfolio model that compromised the strategic insights and distorted the allocation of resources, to the cash cows, problem children and stars in the portfolio of products.

Since then I have evolved my thinking with the support of many collaborators, co-authors, colleagues and clients, and built upon the broad advances in the fields of marketing and strategy. During this journey I have accumulated many debts, well beyond what can properly be recognized here, so I truly hope my debts to them will be partly repaid by their recognition and citation throughout this book. A special acknowl-edgment is due to my friends and close colleagues Paul Schoemaker, Tom Donaldson and Harbir Singh, and to the extended community of the Mack Institute for Innovation Management at the Wharton School.

Above all, I am grateful for the inspiration and support of my dear wife, Alice, who sustained me during this writing journey. This book is dedi-cated to her.

George S. Day
Villanova, Pennsylvania
2022

# 1    Marketing strategy: the guiding premises

Marketing functions at the interface of a business and its markets, and absorbs a great deal of the turbulence in those markets. This turbulence keeps mounting as all markets have been assailed by a global pandemic, trade uncertainties, and the digital transformation of every business activity. How does a well-conceived marketing strategy help a business navigate this turbulence and make the right decisions, to ensure the organization can accomplish its performance objectives? The answer depends on what is meant by "marketing" and "strategy."

*What is marketing?* There is no straightforward answer, because marketing plays a variety of roles with activities that are increasingly shared within the organization (Webster 1992) or with partners. There are three distinct meanings that are mutually reinforcing, which take different perspectives on the strategic issues of the organization and apply at different levels. Their collective meaning is captured in Figure 1.1.

The first meaning of marketing is that it is a distinctive feature of an organization's culture; an *external orientation and decision approach* putting the understanding and meeting of needs of customers first. This meaning comes with many designations and identities: as a market orientation (or being market driven/focused/driving) or customer orientated (or being a customer centered/focused/led) organization. These are mostly distinctions without a difference (Day 1999). Each has a genesis in Drucker's (1954) insistence, "There is only one valid definition of business purpose: to create a customer ... Concern and responsibility for marketing must therefore permeate all areas of the enterprise."

Marketing is also a *general management responsibility*, for choosing, "where to play" and "how to win" (Lafley and Martin 2013). There are challenging questions, because they require the leadership to make

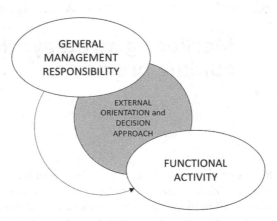

**Figure 1.1**    What does marketing mean?

defensible choices about the future of their organization. The answers are a shared responsibility of the chief executive officer (CEO) and the leadership team. This responsibility is best discharged by approaching these defining choices from the outside in. We delve more deeply into what this means later in this book, and we argue it is better to start the process of making a strategy by first stepping outside the boundaries, resources and constraints of the organization as it is, and viewing it objectively through the eyes of customers, competitors, channel partners and other players in the market.

The third and most visible role of marketing is as a separate *function*, organized around a core set of activities to carry out the market-facing aspects of an outside-in strategy. Since marketing is the most context-dependent function, these activities and their relative importance can range from the go-to-market activities in capital-intensive manufacturing firms to the social media and messaging themes for consumer goods companies. Paradoxically, the deeper marketing is embedded within an organization and customer value leadership becomes the distinguishing theme of the strategy, the more likely the functional role of marketing is likely to be blurred and obscured.

*What is strategy?* There is no agreed-upon definition of strategy that describes the field and limits its boundaries (Freedman 2013), so it has become an elastic term: there is *strategic* supply chain management ..., *strategic* human resources ..., *strategic* (fill in the blank). Sometimes strategies are confused with objectives; for example: "Our strategy is to be the dominant competitor in our markets." Good strategies require integrated and coherent choices about how to achieve the objectives that are set, allocate resources, and align diverse interests and activities throughout the organization. Think of a strategy as a resonating theme that mobilizes the organization.

A strategy expresses the aspirations of a firm and the set of choices that lead to an advantageous position in a market (Porter 1996). Another definition that captures the reality of making strategic choices is, "the alignment of potentially unlimited aspirations with necessarily limited capabilities ... whatever balance you strike, there'll be a link between what's real and what's imagined; between your current location and your intended destination" (Gaddis 2018, p. 21). The kernel of this strategy (Rumelt 2011) has a sound diagnosis of the situation, a guiding policy specifying how the firm will deal with the threats and opportunities identified with this diagnosis, and a coherent set of actions.

*What is marketing strategy?* This is a core aspect of a competitive strategy answering the questions, "where to play?" and "how to win?" by achieving customer value leadership and continually innovating new value for customers. These are the customer value imperatives of a marketing strategy and they focus the firm on creating and profiting from superior customer value. This benefits the firm through superior financial performance and the creation of valuable customer and brand assets. These assets also shape the marketing strategy through actions taken to protect and capitalize on these assets (Day and Moorman 2010). This strategy is formulated from the outside in, and enabled by deep market insights. It works in tandem with the financial, talent and operations strategies. This integrated view of marketing strategy incorporates the orchestration of the resources and capabilities of the form, and expands the domain beyond that which chief marketing officers (CMOs) and marketers spend most of their time and effort in practice (Varadarajan 2010; Morgan et al. 2019).

This perspective on marketing strategy is consistent with the usual distinctions between the *content* of a strategy, the *process* of strategy making, and the *implementation* activities. While these are useful distinctions, they are, in practice, highly interdependent, with the implementation choices both enabling and constraining the strategic choices, and vice versa.

The marketing strategy is the collective responsibility of the leadership team and requires that all parts of the firm's governance and operations – incentives, hiring decisions, outsourcing, partnering and beyond – be aligned to the pursuit of superior customer value. Yet, if everyone in the C-suite is responsible, then no one may be accountable for these choices and actions. Increasingly, firms are facing this reality and holding the CMO or chief commercial officer (CCO) accountable for orchestrating the firm's activities on behalf of customer value.

*Summary.* The benefits of a marketing perspective on strategy depend on the orientation of the firm toward customers, and the emphasis placed by leadership on achieving and sustaining superior customer value. To complete this chapter, we translate these themes into the four guiding premises underpinning this book. They are the product of a path-dependent evolution of the field of marketing, in that we build on what we know. In the next chapter we assess pertinent influences from the past to better appreciate the current state of the field, and then anticipate how marketing should best contribute to strategy formulation when markets are increasingly turbulent.

## Guiding premises

Four guiding premises are the basic building blocks upon which marketing strategies are built, and establish the scope and structure of this book:

- Achieving and sustaining superior customer value is the goal and the integrating theme of a marketing strategy.
- Innovating new value for customers requires the disciplined search and selection of opportunities.
- Strategy-making starts from the outside in.
- Outside-in organizations are better prepared for increasing market turbulence.

### Premise one: achieving and sustaining superior customer value is the goal of a marketing strategy

Customer value is about the trade-off between the benefits customers perceive they get from an offering, versus the perceived total life-cycle costs of these benefits, after adjusting for the riskiness of the offer. The emphases on *perceived benefits* has been imprinted on marketing thinking since Ted Levitt (1960, p. 28) famously observed, "People don't want to buy a quarter-inch drill. They want a quarter-inch hole."

An effective marketing strategy specifies how a business intends to achieve customer value leadership in the market segments it chooses to serve. It is a direction set by three choices:

- *Arena:* the markets to serve and the customer segments to target.
- *Advantage:* the customer value positioning theme that differentiates the business.
- *Activities:* the scale and scope of activities to be performed by the organization or with partners.

These choices are highly interdependent; a change in one means changes in the others.

The pandemic of 2020 accelerated a shift toward a multiple stakeholder model, embracing the concept put forward by the Business Roundtable (2019, p. 2) that, "While each of our individual companies serve its own corporate purpose, we share a fundamental commitment to all of our stakeholders." Received doctrine among marketers (Challagalla et al. 2014), enshrined in slogans such as "Customer is King" is that customer should be *primus inter pares* relative to other stakeholders, implicitly subordinating employees, suppliers, communities and equity shareholders. This message was reinforced during the turnaround of Procter & Gamble (P&G) when A.G. Lafley became CEO in 2009. He found a demoralized organization where the pace of innovation had declined dramatically. To center the organization, he adopted the mantra "Consumer is boss." With intense repetition and his personal commitment, Lafley was able to embed this notion into the cultural values of the company. Despite the success of the P&G turnaround, and decades of endorsement, there is still resistance to the primacy of the customer in the stakeholder model.

## Premise two: innovating new value for customer requires discipline

Why are some firms consistently able to grow faster than their direct rivals? First, growth leaders follow a disciplined outside-in approach to probing all the possible growth pathways to identify the best opportunities, choose among them carefully, and then implement those that best serve the growth strategy. They eschew a reactive posture that waits for the opportunities to come to them or emerge from the firm's technology development process. A full-spectrum approach to growth stretches and reimagines every dimension of the customer value proposition and the enabling business model.

Growth leaders maintain a healthy tension between the creative, risk-taking and experimenting part of the innovation process, and the disciplined, rigorous and results-orientated part. An innovative organization needs both right-brained and left-brained functions. If one side dominates, overall innovation performance will suffer. When exploratory and creative thinking are emphasized, ideas will flow, but the development process will be clogged with too many projects competing for scarce resources.

Discipline is also exercised by the leadership team when they accept well-intentioned failures, occurring for unexpected and unforeseen reasons, and emphasize drawing lessons from these failures to improve the process and the next round of innovations. Without this tolerance and ability to learn, the people proposing new ways to deliver value to customers will avoid risk; they will be encouraged to play it safe and keep a low profile. This creates a conservative, fault-finding culture that subverts the innovation process.

## Premise three: strategy making starts from the outside in

The essence of an outside-in approach to strategy formulation is an iterative learning process, initiated with wide-angle scanning and sensing of the environment. The benefits of this approach are most fully realized within a supportive organization with four defining properties. The first property is a leadership team endorsing this approach as a decision-making priority, and embracing it within their mental model. This leadership commitment is fully realized within an empathetic organization that is catalyzed by collective curiosity and supported with a system-wide emphasis on gaining insight.

This approach to strategy formulation will not produce superior performance unless it is grounded in deep market insights. An insight is a "new understanding of some facet of marketplace change that makes a difference" (Fahey 2018, p. 2). Insights are a means to an end, not an end in themselves. They should inform and encourage deeper thinking and yield better and earlier decisions that can be implemented. They are an antidote to formulaic thinking and business-as-usual approaches. Genuine market insights are novel; to be valuable they cannot be common knowledge. Valuable insights are obtained with a diversity of inputs, which helps overcome the centripetal pull of inside-out thinking.

## Premise four: outside-in organizations are better prepared

Marketing has never been more complex, and the future will be even more turbulent. Sweeping advances in digital technologies are transforming markets and the practice of marketing. Societal issues emerging from the climate crisis, inequality and the aftershocks of the pandemic are increasing uncertainty. Consumers are becoming more concerned about the wider consequences for their consumption choices, and gravitate toward less wasteful products. This is probably an enduring generational change, as younger consumers are driving this shift in priorities. These societal shifts are interacting with, and being accentuated by, digital and e-everything: e-browsing, e-shopping, e-payments and e-media consumption. These profound changes are paralleling changes in the role of the CMO, and abetted by new organizational designs. The emerging marketing organization will be more customer-centric, composed of smaller structural units and highly networked both inside and outside the firm.

Market-driven organizations that approach their strategy making from the outside in, are much better prepared to anticipate and adapt to this cascade of societal changes and stay ahead of digital advances. The properties of outside-in organizations feature an empathetic orientation, catalyzed by collective curiosity, while building superior foresight capabilities. These outside-in organizations behave more like "foxes," with wide-ranging curiosity, than "hedgehogs" who know one big thing and extend the explanatory reach of that one big thing to new domains. Tetlock (2005) found that foxes were far more proficient predictors, because they stitched together diverse sources of partial information, instead of relying on deduction from unquestioned mental models. Turbulent markets are best navigated by foxes who ensure their organizations are better prepared.

## Persistent dilemmas shaping marketing strategy

Some of the best thinking on strategy making comes when practice illuminates theory, and vice versa. Progress is made when there is a robust and mutually informed, two-way dialogue between thoughtful practitioners and theorists. Not only are managers in new practice companies at the leading edge of developing issues, but their ongoing experimentation with ways to address these issues yields valuable theories-in-use that are the basis for more general explanations. A theory-in-use is a manager's mental model of how things work in a particular context (Zeithaml et al. 2020), envisioned as a set of if-then relationships among actions and outcomes. The managers become co-creators of a situational theory, by sharing their beliefs about the constructs that matter, and practices that work. This is an especially useful approach when the constructs are ambiguous and/or practice is changing.

Further progress also means the field will tackle the persistent dilemmas that create pulls from seemingly opposite directions. These dilemmas were first identified by Prahalad (1995) when he characterized the state of research as a silent, ongoing battle between weak signals from practice and well-developed paradigms in fields of scholarly inquiry. The following are among the most entrenched and intractable dilemmas shaping strategic marketing.

*Strategy content versus process.* There are two camps here, making different assumptions. The strategy content camp uses rigorous modeling and large data-sets to study well-defined issues. By contrast, the process camp sees strategy making as a complex stream of trial-and-error moves, reactions and reflections rather than discrete choices. Strategy process research is akin to streaming video, whereas strategy content research is most often a still image. While strategy content and process should be complementary, they are usually studied separately. Within the totality of marketing strategy research the process of making strategy is rarely investigated (Morgan et al. 2019). This imbalance is problematic as, according to the process point of view, strategies are more likely to emerge from piecemeal, interim responses to events over which management has little control, than through the analytical process of matching opportunities with capabilities. Mintzberg (1994) summed up this perspective by arguing that strategy making requires insight, creativity and learning. In this view the world is too complex and uncertain to allow strategies to be formulated all at once. Instead, a strategy emerges in small steps as an organization learns and adapts.

*Rules versus exceptions.* An enduring question is how to interpret empirical findings when they are distorted by industry rules. The observed results of strategic moves reflect behavior constrained by industry rules, norms, and conventional wisdom, and are susceptible to a survivor bias. We are usually unable to observe the results of either failed processes or strategies. Not only are we mostly studying organizations that survive, but the resulting theories are based on those firms that survive and are willing to be studied. Another problem is that any first-order economic law, such as "invest to increase market share in rapid growth markets" cannot be acted upon as it contradicts the economic principle of rational expectations. Since everyone can be expected to use this general rule in the same way, it does not offer a basis for differentiation. This is leading scholars and insightful entrepreneurs to seek exceptions to the general rules.

*Objective versus enacted reality.* The normative strategy literature implicitly assumes that market environments are objective and waiting to be discovered, and that managers are rational and well-informed information processors, using their conceptual frameworks to formulate and choose strategies. This assumption is being challenged by a revisionist view that what matters is how managers interpret their environment in the mental models they use to simplify and make sense of their environment (Senge 2006). Proponents argue that constructs such as markets, segments, competitive force, and entry barriers are abstractions given meaning through processes of selective search and attention, selective perception, and simplification. These processes are shared through industry conventional wisdom, warped by functional biases and tempered by the ready availability of data. Thus far this competing view has had little influence on research in marketing strategy, despite persuasive evidence that these enactments of reality matter.

*Established versus embryonic markets.* Strategy researchers are most comfortable studying established markets where the product features are known, customers usage patterns can be observed, and the market is (reasonably) specifiable. There are many concepts and procedures for analyzing consumer trade-offs using conjoint analysis, identifying competitive forces with industry structure analysis, and developing incremental new products with stage-gate systems.

We are less secure with emerging markets being created or transformed by disruptive or radical innovations, such as recombinant deoxyribonucleic acid (DNA), facial recognition, machine learning or crypto-currencies, in a bewildering array of combinations. These are such a different game, with their evolution beset by uncertainty, that available concepts and methods are poorly suited.

*General versus contingent.* There is an implicit, and sometimes overt, presumption that marketing strategy is the responsibility of the CMO and the marketing team. This is only reasonable if there is a CMO or CCO with credibility and membership in the C-suite. However (as we discuss in the Appendix to this book), it is more likely that the marketing function serves more as a market advocate (bringing the voice of the customer to the organization) or a service resource, than a true top-line leader. What is needed is a contingency theory to explain this variance in roles and assert the reality that the best way to devise and implement a marketing strategy depends on the situation. This is a longstanding and durable issue in the field of strategy.

## My plan for this book

The terms "plans" and "planning" have not been used thus far, so why now? In some circles these terms have fallen into disrepute and elicit a sense of overly linear, formalized and unimaginative thinking. Yet, strategic processes and choices must eventually yield plans that formalize the consequences: budgets, resource allocations, staffing priorities, and so on, supported with responsibilities and time lines. That is, these plans lay out the details of how the goals and choices will be attained.

The sequencing and scope of the chapter plan for this book is the realization of my objectives for this book, the choice of topics and how each is treated, and most importantly how I meet your needs as a reader/consumer. Here is what you can expect as we explore more deeply the four guiding premises: (1) the primacy of superior customer value, (2) the need to continually innovate new value for customers because advantages are increasingly transitory, (3) starting the strategy-making process with a wide lens, outside-in approach, and (4) building an outside-in organization to better prepare for increasing market turbulence.

Chapter 2, "Marketing strategy: looking back to see ahead," completes the introduction to the topics of this book by looking back to the evolution of the adjacent fields of strategy and strategy making, to appreciate why the influence of marketing has waned, albeit from a high level. The antidotes that could bring marketing strategy back to a more central role are a renewed emphasis on marketing excellence that meets the needs for organizations to navigate ever more turbulent markets. The sources of this turbulence are suggested by the main zones of uncertainty that collectively create potential opportunities as well as looming threats in the future.

Chapter 3 on "Achieving customer value leadership," develops the central theme or organizing principle of a marketing strategy. This chapter addresses two defining questions. The first is, "What is customer value?" The answer is a customer value equation that specifies the trade-off between the perceived benefits and the perceived costs, adjusted for the riskiness of the offer. The second question is, "How do customers choose?" The answer is represented by the value vector model that reflects the trade-offs between three types of value: performance, price, and relational. The underlying message of this chapter is that customer value leaders do not succeed by being, "all things to all customers." Strategy formulation is about making choices.

Chapter 4 asks an even tougher question: "How do customer value leaders sustain their advantage?" When markets are evolving at a faster pace and customer value priorities are changing, there is a constant threat of commoditization, so it is becoming more difficult to sustain value leadership. Outside-in strategists have answers, based on deep insights into the forces of value erosion and a willingness to make audacious defensive moves. These responses mean mobilizing a business model to deliver and capture the customer value.

Chapters 5 and 6 address two challenges to customer value leaders: (1) the increasing rate of erosion of their value advantage under relentless competitive pressure, and (2) the economic imperative to grow faster organically than their rivals. We show how organic growth leaders use a disciplined approach to finding their best opportunities and pursuing them ahead of others. They don't wait for opportunities to emerge before reacting. Instead they systematically explore the possibilities for innovation revealed by stretching and reimagining every dimension of their strategy. Growth leaders balance *divergence* – to widen their search across the full spectrum of 12 possible growth pathways – with *convergence* on those that best support their growth strategy. These leaders also know that the less traveled growth pathways may offer opportunities for innovation that can change the basis of competition.

In Chapters 7 and 8 we turn from understanding the content of customer value leadership strategies, to the iterative process by which they are formulated. This shift in perspective helps to better understand the outside-in approach, as an iterative learning process, initiated with wide-angle scanning and sensing of the environment. The benefits of this approach are fully realized within a supportive organization that has four defining properties. The first property is a leadership team adopting this approach as a decision-making priority and embracing it as their mental model. This leadership commitment is fully realized within an empathetic organization that is catalyzed by collective curiosity and supported with a system-wide emphasis on gaining foresight.

The purpose of Chapter 9 is to re-emphasize the central role of an effective marketing organization in ensuring there is an informed outside-in perspective during the strategy dialogue. Meanwhile, marketing organizations are being transformed by digital technologies and increasing market turbulence. These profound changes are occurring in tandem with changes in the role of the CMO and abetted by new organizational designs. The emerging marketing organization will be more customer-centric. Within this evolved organization, the priorities for the marketing leader will be to build superior marketing capabilities, integrate digital technologies ahead of competitors, tighten the alignment with sales, and take accountability for the returns on marketing investments.

## Summary

Our guiding premises will serve as foundational themes and handrails for readers to stay in tune with the plan for this book. The core themes of achieving and sustaining superior customer value, and starting the strategy dialogue from the outside in, pervade and anchor each chapter. When these themes are firmly in place, the organization will be better prepared to navigate the market turbulence that is sure to increase.

# 2 Marketing strategy: looking back to see ahead

Histories serve many functions. They reveal our origins, celebrate our successes and remind us of our debts to our intellectual forbears. Histories also help to interpret the past by identifying the reasons for important transitions. They may provide clues about the future. If we project where the current momentum is carrying the field of marketing strategy, then some troubling questions arise. The ancient Chinese saying, "Unless we change our direction, we are likely to wind up where we are headed," is a warning. However, momentum is neither irreversible nor irresistible, and many forces will shape further progress.

A compressed history of scholarship and thinking about competitive strategies over the past 50 years shows four phases of evolution, beginning in the early 1970s with research on the outcomes of strategic choices and working back along the "food chain" to study the sources of the advantages that were gained. Throughout this evolutionary process the aim was to understand how firms behave and why they are different (Rumelt et al. 1994). From this stream of research, strategy was defined as the match between what a firm could do with its strengths and weaknesses, given the threats and opportunities in the environment. However, managers were given little guidance on how to assess either side of the equation.

During *phase one* of the development of systematic approaches to strategy, the focus was largely on *the performance outcomes* of strategy. In this early work much was made of portfolio models that prescribed market share strategies based on market attractiveness and business strength, such as the growth-share matrix developed by Bruce Henderson and the Boston Consulting Group. The experience curve relationship of costs with cumulative output was a significant building block, and so the relationship of market share and profitability became a matter of heated debate. This entailed the search for the underlying or third factor influencing both share and profits.

Toward the end of this first phase, industry structure analysis became influential through Michael Porter's (1980) work on competitive strategy. His model of the "five forces" of competition built on the structure-conduct-performance paradigm of industrial organization economics. The emphasis of this approach was on understanding the industry context, and finding attractive positions within the industry that minimized direct rivalry.

The *second phase* shifted attention to the *positional advantages* the firm had created in order to achieve lower delivered costs or superior customer value through differentiation. This phase peaked in the mid to late 1980s and led to active interest in strategic typologies, generic strategies, and the dimensions of advantage such as quality or channel relations. Research on the Profit Impact of Market Strategy (PIMS) database (Buzzell and Gale 1987) helped clarify the importance of relative quality, as a measure of differentiation, and demonstrated there was not a cost penalty from higher quality levels. There was increasing use of economic theory, ranging from transaction cost analyses of integration and governance questions, to game theoretic studies of entry and exit strategies and the influence of producer reputations.

A *third phase* emerged in the 1980s as the focus shifted from outside to inside the firm. The shift in attention to the *sources* of advantage was a recognition that positional and performance superiority achieved in the market was derived from relative superiority in the skills, assets, collective learning, and prevailing values and culture embedded in the firm, and the ability of management to mobilize them (Collis and Montgomery 1995). This was belated recognition that what really matters is the specific actions that management takes to innovate in products and processes, enhance product and service quality, shorten time-to-market, and build strong customer and channel relationships.

The transition to phase three was signaled by the enthusiastic reception given to the concepts of core competence (Prahalad and Hamel 1990) and competing on capabilities. Since capabilities proved so difficult to identify, most attention was on self-contained aspects, such as coordinating diverse production skills, harmonizing streams of technology, and organizing work processes. This proved a very internal view of competencies, susceptible to a circular logic that dealt with only a part of the chain of causality. The early work stopped at the point of observing that successful businesses out-perform their rivals because they have superior resources (Porter 1991) – hardly a solid basis for prescription. These problems are being addressed by specifying the conditions under which capabilities are valuable, such as scarcity (is it imitable or substitutable, and is it durable?) and appropriability (who owns the profits?). This led to a significant stream of research on the sustainability of competitive advantages.

The interest in capabilities exercised within processes and the associated resource-based view (RBV) of the firm (Barney and Clark 2007) fit well with the emphasis of the early 1990s on delayering, restructuring, and reengineering, since they required reconceiving the firm as a collection of linked processes. The basis of the RBV is that scarce, inimitable, and valuable resources exist to be used, and the task of management is to improve and fully exploit these resources (Makadok 2001). This leads to an emphasis on internal efficiency improvements and short-term cost reductions. As a starting point for strategic thinking, however, it myopically narrows and anchors the dialogue prematurely. Nonetheless, the RBV continues to influence marketing thinking (Kozlenkova et al. 2013).

A *fourth phase*, built on the cumulative insights gained during the progression from:

Performance Outcomes ⇒ Positional Advantages ⇒ Sources of Advantage

This phase coincided with growing doubts about the pursuit of sustainable competitive advantage as a strategic priority. The "end of competitive advantage" was pronounced (McGrath 2013), or more precisely the end of defensible, permanent, and durable advantages. The emerging theme of transient, temporary, and short-lived advantages was presaged by D'Aveni (1994), who addressed hypercompetitive market environments in which advantages are rapidly created or eroded.

There have been ongoing concerns about ambiguity of the notion of competitive advantage. Did it mean, achieving the highest profit, above-average profit, positive economic profit, the low-cost position, or the largest value gap in a segment or market? We should regard competitive advantage as a conceptual umbrella. It is also contended that the introduction of value-gap concepts (where a competitive advantage is a gap between customer value and cost that is larger than the gap of competitors) has compounded these ambiguities. In the next chapter, we see that the value-gap concept is flawed and susceptible to inside-out thinking.

The core of these contrarian positions was that basing strategy on the search for sustainable competitive advantages has become less meaningful for most companies. Instead of extracting maximum value from competitive advantages, companies should emphasize their capacity to "surf through waves of short-lived opportunities" (McGrath 2013, p. 20). In an environment of temporary advantages, firms need to be able to reconfigure themselves continually, and dynamically renew their advantages. The enabler for this process is provided by dynamic capabilities that create, adjust, and keep relevant the stock of capabilities.

*Dynamic capabilities* enable organizational fitness and help shape the environment advantageously by (1) sensing organizational changes that could be threats or opportunities by scanning, searching, and exploring across markets and technologies, (2) responding to the changes by combining and transforming available resources in new and different ways or even adding new resources through alliance partnerships or acquisitions, and (3) selecting the organizational configuration and business model for delivering economic value to customers, and then capturing the economic profit (Teece 2009). A dynamic capability is not an ad hoc solution to a problem, but a repeatable and deeply embedded set of skills and knowledge exercised through processes. An example of dynamic capabilities in action is the way IBM took its existing competencies in technology and quality, and added to them the capability to learn better how to serve their customers' needs, transforming from a product company to one that integrates systems to solve customers' problems (Harreld et al. 2007).

During this fourth phase and into the present, the field of strategy has returned to its roots and emphasized the role of purpose – the core reason for being – that clarifies what a business stands for and is aspirational. The aim is to reshape the value proposition and widen the scope to include the broader ecosystem. Within marketing, Vargo and Lusch (2004, 2017) advocated a transition from a goods-centered to a service-centered logic that emphasized solutions that expand markets by assisting the consumer in the process of value co-creation. While this service-dominant (S-D) logic (as it is known) holds promise of providing an expanded and integrative view of marketing, its current development seems confined to an interdisciplinary group of service researchers (Fehrer 2020).

## Influences on strategy making

Concerns about marketing's influence were first raised in Day (1992) with a forecast that the trajectory of slow erosion of the strategic role of marketing (albeit from a high level) might be reversed. The reasons were grounded in the fit of the issues, trends, and fashions in strategy making with the distinctive knowledge, skills, and competencies of marketers. When the fit is close, then marketing gains influence by contributing superior insights. As the fit loosens and/or other disciplines and functions are more attuned to emerging issues, then marketing loses relative influence during the strategy dialogue. These concerns have been made episodically from the 1990s to date, for diverse reasons.

Within firms, the direct influence of marketing on the strategy dialogue has diminished for two good reasons. Among market leaders, market orientation or customer-centricity attitudes and behaviors have been infused throughout the organization and embedded deeply within the culture. Meanwhile, the locus of strategy making is shifting to the leadership team, with the support of a strategy group. The influential members of this team are strong communicators with sound judgment, serving as credible advisors to the chief executive officer (CEO) on strategic issues. Significantly more than advocates for their functional group, they are team players who can overcome their natural tendency to protect the interests of their functional silo and focus on immediate tasks. As marketing leaders subsume their functional biases and evolve to being team members, they face challenges from rapid digital advances, intensifying competition, and orchestrating an integrated customer experience. Meanwhile, academic marketing has not kept up. Among the reasons (Reibstein et al. 2009; Key et al. 2020; Wierenga 2020) are:

- A shrinking domain, owing to pre-emption of marketing frameworks, concepts, and methods by adjacent fields of academic enquiry.
- The inherent limitations of reductionist, narrowly specified and fragmented research studies are ill-suited to the dynamic, multifaceted problems of managers.
- The predominant academic research paradigm begins with a new methodology, data-set or behavioral hypothesis, rather than starting with a managerial problem. This leads to a variant of the "streetlight effect" (Du et al. 2021) on enquiries, owing to an overreliance on what is readily available.

A possible antidote to this degradation is a renewed emphasis on *marketing excellence* (Moorman and Day 2016; Homburg et al. 2020). Excellence is defined as a superior ability to carry out essential customer-facing activities that enhance performance, especially emphasizing organic growth achieved through sustainable revenue increases. This excellence is achieved through an organization's marketing culture, capabilities, and configuration, and these in turn influence the seven key marketing activities in the marketing-strategy process.

These seven As (7As) comprise the contributions of marketing to: *Anticipating* marketplace changes; *Adapting* the firm to such changes; *Aligning* processes, structures, and people; *Activating* efficient and effective individual and organizational behaviors; creating *Accountability* for marketing performance; *Attracting* important financial, human, and other resources; and engaging in *Asset management* that develops and deploys marketing assets.

Activities are the basic ingredients of organizations and are central to strategy, beginning with value-chain analysis and strategy maps (Porter 1996) and advancing to the contemporary view that organizations are systems composed of choices of activities that interact to create a competitive advantage (Zott and Amit 2007). The field of marketing treats the concept of activities very loosely, with the activities ascribed to marketing mostly confined to the four Ps (4Ps) of product, price, place, and promotion. This narrow framework fails to capture many of the vital roles that marketing plays. Mastery of the seven activities is essential for marketing to fully contribute to the strategy dialogue. Their functions and roles are woven throughout this book.

## Looking toward a more turbulent future

Marketing grew up in an era of manageable uncertainty, where the future was relatively predictable and changes were more measured. The mental models and organization designs favored by many current marketers are a legacy of this era. Most marketing strategy models and efficiency-orientated tactical moves are still predicated on a modicum of predictability of technological, socioeconomic and geopolitical trends (Rust 2020).

Uncertainty comes from not knowing with confidence which forces and trends will matter in the future. The possible outcomes and/or the probabilities of these forces occurring are unknown. It is tempting to project past trends forward, but experience reminds us that these projections will not be the biggest shapers of the future. Instead, the future will emerge through the resolution of a myriad of uncertainties. Even seemingly inexorable technological trends can create uncertainty owing to the unpredictability of simultaneous advances in complementary digital technologies, sharp declines in their costs, new functionalities, and new platforms that put them to work (Day and Schoemaker 2019).

A scenario approach is needed to reveal and organize the underlying uncertainties. Scenario learning is a way of rehearsing the future to avoid surprises by breaking through the "illusion of certainty" (Fahey and Randall 1998). Unlike traditional strategic planning, which presumes there is a most probable answer to a strategic issue, scenario learning considers multiple plausible futures. It meets the needs of marketers for plans, capabilities, and organizational models that are robust across the scenarios that reflect uncertain market realities.

The scenarios for the alternative plausible future roles of marketing in strategy making will be synthesized from the interaction of many uncertainties. In a VUCA (military acronym for volatility, uncertainty, complexity, and ambiguity) world there are diverse and multiplying sources of uncertainty. Those are clustered into the six zones of uncertainty in Figure 2.1. They are informed by in-depth interviews with senior leaders, participation in a network of chief strategy officers, informed speculation by futurists, and ongoing studies of the capabilities of vigilant organizations (Day and Schoemaker 2019, 2021; Schoemaker and Day 2020). The arrows linking the zones suggest some of the combinations and interactions that could magnify systemic uncertainty. Each industry and firm will experience the possible threats and opportunities from these uncertainties differently. Our purpose in discussing each of the six zones is not to be exhaustive, but to suggest the depth and ambition of a creative consideration of the possibilities.

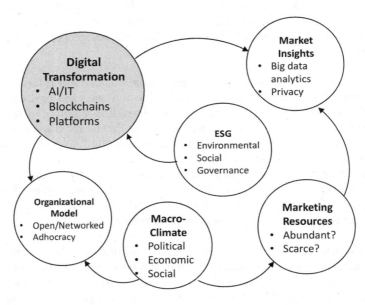

**Figure 2.1**    Illustrative zones of uncertainty for market

*Digital transformation.* It is presumptive to imagine what is ahead for digital technologies, as we can never foresee human ingenuity. However, on the horizon, advances in artificial intelligence, the Internet of things, and blockchains will underpin an infrastructure where marketing activities will be experiential and instantaneous in a constant loop (Kumar 2021) that marketers can tap into to create an integrated customer experience. Meanwhile artificial intelligence (AI) platforms, search engines, and digital assistants, such as Alexa, are populating homes and changing how companies connect with their customers (Dawar and Bendle 2018).

*ESG (environmental, social, and governance).* The environment is the looming climate crisis that threatens to constrain and override every strategy move. One of the consequences is the impetus given to circular business models that extend the lifespan of products through reuse, repair, upgrading, and proactive maintenance (Frishamman and Parida 2019).

*Market insights.* The uncertainties of digital enablement and ESG clash to potentially erode the value of customer data. The way this data is gathered, used and regulated has changed tremendously (Brodherson et al. 2021). Tracking tools have dramatically increased both the sophistication of personalization of advertising messages and the potential for violating consumer privacy. Few consumers believe companies will use their personal data responsibly, so governments will continue to impose limits on the use of the data.

*Organizational model.* There is considerable uncertainty about whether the familiar self-contained, hierarchical model can adjust to rising turbulence. The main argument for its continued prevalence is that it has shown it can adapt. Shortcomings have sometimes been overcome by patches, such as matrices or coordinating functions. The converse position is that the forces of inertia, embedded in legacy systems and mental models, will be too resistant to change. The principle alternatives to the traditional model are the open network approach and the adhocracy where action is privileged over formal position and individual knowledge (Birkinshaw and Ridderstrale 2017). This latter model also requires a new view of strategy based on real options and learning from experimentation.

*Marketing resources.* Will these resources be abundant or scarce? This will depend on the biggest zone of uncertainty, the economic climate. We experienced extreme volatility in demand during the pandemic, with shortages and inflation further clouding the climate. A future environment of scarce resources and short-term thinking forces marketing activities into a defensive mode and strengthens the sales function which delivers short-run revenue. Conversely, in an abundant environment where profits are expanding, top-line growth is a higher priority and longer horizons encourage riskier investments. This is a more favorable setting for marketing to exercise strategic leadership.

*Macro climate.* Global enterprises have prospered for decades thanks to a supportive environment of falling trade barriers, protected financial systems, adequate social and political stability, and rapid advances in digital technologies. However, blithe assumptions about continued economic progress have been upended by a series of geopolitical shocks and the pandemic. Deceptive stability has been replaced with mounting turbulence, political discontent, growing uncertainty, and leadership anxiety. Recall the havoc wrought by the deep financial crisis of 2008, populist autocratic leaders rising in many countries, a fast-spreading global pandemic, trade wars with China, and the continuing cybersecurity breaches. These shocks introduce systemic uncertainty in every other zone of uncertainty. The antidote is to build a superior capability to anticipate, understand, and respond to whatever may be coming over the horizon.

## Looking ahead

The centrality of superior customer value to an outside-in strategy begs the questions of not just how to achieve value leadership, but why it should be the goal at all! For 50 years (Friedman 1970) the accepted goal of a firm has been to maximize shareholder value. The enduring appeal of this goal is a tribute to the elegance of the argument, and the speed of the feedback from the equity markets on whether the goal has been achieved. The reality is that shareholder value, as measured by equity prices, is almost entirely a reflection of the market's expectations of future earnings, and this, in turn, is a consequence of the firm's ability to create new value for customers and grow faster.

Is it appropriate to rank the stakeholders in importance? We believe that they are co-equal, and each contributes to the health of the firm within a reinforcing system. A better approach is to select where to start to improve this system. To guide this choice, consider the robust correlation between employee and customer satisfaction (Zeithhaml 2000; Chamberlain and Zhao 2019), which reveals a reciprocal relationship, where an improvement in the satisfaction of one stakeholder encourages the other to improve. The clear implication is that employee satisfaction should be the starting point. This reinforces the meaning of strategies as integrated actions throughout the organization that deliver superior customer value to the chosen markets.

# 3  Achieving customer value leadership[1]

Astride every competitive market are one or more leaders in market share, profitability, and customer retention that confidently deliver superior value to their target customers. They are able to maximize the benefits perceived by their target customers, while minimizing the perceived costs and risks, relative to their rivals. That is, they have a superior customer value proposition (Payne et al. 2017).

The customer value proposition (CVP) has been termed the essence of marketing strategy and, "the firm's most important single organizing principle" (Webster 2002, p. 61). The value proposition canvas is widely used by firms to rethink and refresh their strategy (Osterwalder et al. 2014), and insure there is a fit between what is needed and what is possible. Becoming a customer value leader defines the strategic direction of a business, shapes the investments the firm must make, and the capabilities to be acquired, developed and nurtured.

There is more than one way to be a customer value leader, since customers perceive value in different ways and have different requirements. An outside-in approach is based on a deep understanding of the value priorities of a target market segment. The ensuing value position is what customers, competitors, and channel partners see, and determines what is chosen by customers. In this chapter we describe a theoretically grounded and usable concept of customer value, then discuss how customers make choices based on their value priorities. This will never be a static picture, so we then describe the dynamic forces creating the movie of changes in CVPs. Marketing leaders need to have a well-informed view of the impact of these forces and how they will shape the business model that delivers the value proposition.

## What is customer value?

*Perceptions of relative perceived value* drive customer choices, their subsequent satisfaction and loyalty, and the word-of-mouth and social media recommendations these customers make. Ultimately, customer value is about the trade-off between the benefits that customers perceive they are receiving from a product or service, and the perceived cost of obtaining these benefits – adjusted for the riskiness of the offer, as shown in this equation:

Customer Value = (1 – Perceived Risk) [Perceived Customer Benefits – Perceived Life Cycle Costs]

Each of the components has been the subject of much scholarly enquiry, the focus of many consulting papers, and needs to be thoroughly understood before a strategy can be formulated. This equation requires judgments that are deeply informed by market insights for many reasons. First, it is crucial to not confuse benefits with features and, second, customers vary greatly in their perceptions of risk, benefits, and costs, and how they judge their relative importance. This equation has to be estimated and understood for each segment in the served market.

### Perceived risk

The degree of risk the prospective buyer perceives depends (Mitchell 1999; Zhang and Yu 2020) on the buyer's uncertainty about the answers to crucial questions, such as: can I trust the buyer's promises? Will the service/product perform as expected? Will the supplier stay in business and support the product in the future? Small vendors with unknown brand names and no track records are at a real disadvantage – hence, the plight of many start-ups.

The diagnostic framework in Figure 3.1 is best used to reveal the areas where medium to high risks are perceived, when evaluating a vendor, which then launches a search for strategic moves to reduce the risk. Creative possibilities for countering a customer segment's perceived risks include:

- *Performance risk.* The potential customer may be afraid the offering will not perform as promised. To allay these concerns, have an inde-

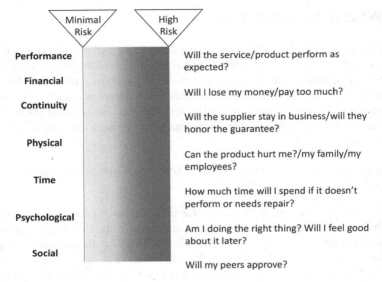

| | Minimal Risk | High Risk | |
|---|---|---|---|
| Performance | | | Will the service/product perform as expected? |
| Financial | | | Will I lose my money/pay too much? |
| Continuity | | | Will the supplier stay in business/will they honor the guarantee? |
| Physical | | | Can the product hurt me?/my family/my employees? |
| Time | | | How much time will I spend if it doesn't perform or needs repair? |
| Psychological | | | Am I doing the right thing? Will I feel good about it later? |
| Social | | | Will my peers approve? |

**Figure 3.1**    Diagnosing customer perceived risk

pendent source conduct tests; share direct feature comparisons with the competitors; offer a warranty or guarantee and share the data on warranty claims. Solicit endorsements by credible authorities, such as key opinion lenders.

- *Financial risk.* This is an issue for high-technology products where price declines follow technology advances, so consider an upgrade or trade-in feature, or even a price guarantee.
- *Continuity risk.* Customers are usually concerned that a start-up will not stay in business, so one option is to partner with a well-known firm in the same market space. (Be careful to consider the strategy of the prospective partner, and whether they really want a joint venture or an acquisition.)
- *Physical and time risk.* Be sure the offering meets or exceeds all government and industry safety standards, and educate your customers about safe product use with seminars, newsletters and product guide. Make the repair or replacement process transparent and seamless.
- *Psychological and social risk.* The more conspicuous the product the greater these risks. To minimize these perceived risk factors reach out to opinion leaders for their endorsement, and ensure the salesforce is seen as knowledgeable and professional.

These perceived risk factors will differ between individuals and product categories. The relative weight of performance and physical risk of an mRNA vaccine for Covid-19 protection will be very different from the factors considered for a new enterprise software application. However, a common theme across categories is the value of delivering a superior customer buying and using experience which will allay any negative perceptions.

## Perceived benefits

There is a crucial difference between benefits and features or attributes, even though they are two sides of the same coin. *Features* describe what an offering is or does. They are attributes such as an electric razor with a five-bladed head, or a memory device with 16 GB of storage. *Benefits* are the outcomes or results that users will obtain – how the offering helps them solve their problems. For example, the technical features of 16 GB of memory enables the benefit of "holding more than 11 000 pictures." A benefits perspective is the core of outside-in thinking. Features are necessary to deliver these benefits, but represent inside-out thinking. On its own a features perspective will seldom yield deep insights into what customers want or how they make choices.

A useful conceptualization of benefits is provided by the value pyramid in which Almquist et al. (2016) describe 30 elements of value (corresponding to benefits) that meet four types of need states – functional, emotional, life changing, and social impact. These needs were derived through a laddering interview technique that probes consumer's stated preferences to identify the underlying reasons for these choices. They found that an emotional benefit, such as reducing anxiety, could be as important as a functional benefit, such as saving time. The elements are ordered in a pyramid, akin to Maslow's hierarchy of needs with very basic needs (security, warmth, food, and rest) at the base and more complex needs (self-esteem and altruism) at the top.

The insights from this value pyramid that are most valuable for formulating strategy are, first, that the functional elements at the base (such as variety, reduces effort, saves time, organizes, and integrates) are easier to measure, and consequently they are easier to match by rivals. Second, companies with strong value propositions score high (8, 9 or 10 on a scale of degree of descriptiveness) on multiple elements of value. Third, companies that excel on multiple elements have higher net promoter scores (NPS), which distinguish customers who are promoters, passives or detractors. Despite the popularity of NPS metric (Colvin 2020) owing to its simplicity, there are numerous flaws, including a disregard of segment differences.

### Customer value creation

The creation of customer value occurs throughout the stages of the customer journey (Payne et al. 2020): (stage 1) pre-exchange activities occur during the process of searching, evaluating and deciding, (stage 2) during the interactions needed to complete the exchange, and (stage 3) post-exchange activities, including the service/repair experience and eventual disposal. Different forms of value are evinced during these states, and are market-context dependent.

## Customer value priorities

Customers want as much value as they can get: "Give me outstanding products, wide selection, knowledgeable service, at the lowest price." They also recognize that they have to make trade-offs and prioritize the dimensions of value to make the best choice. These trade-offs emphasize one of three categories of value: performance value, price value or relational value. Customers tend to sort themselves into segments based on the type of value that is most important to them. This triad is derived from the inside-out framework of Treacy and Wiersema (1997), which was turned outside-in to express the customer's viewpoint (Day and Moorman 2010). Customer value leaders deliver superior value to one of these three segments, with a business model tightly suited to this purpose, while being competitive in the other types of value.

*Performance value.* The main concern of customers emphasizing this type of value is whether the offering is best at meeting their demanding requirements. This may mean having the highest quality, the best functionality, or the most innovative performance features. They are drawn to firms such as Apple computers, Tesla cars or Nike footwear. One of the defining features of this segment is an emphasis on peerless quality, for which they are willing to pay a premium. This is quality, not in the narrow sense of compliance with standards, but in the broad sense of fitness for use. For medical-device makers, such as pacemakers, this means reliability (variance in mean time before malfunction and longevity) since it is both costly and risky to replace a failed pacemaker in the chest cavity.

*Price value.* The priority for this price value segment is obtaining the best price for an acceptable level of performance, service, and relational value. Their emphasis is on the perceived total cost component of the customer value equation. These customers are acutely aware of prices, base their search criteria on relative price, seek bargains relentlessly, and consult with diverse sources when comparison shopping. Their finely honed price sensitivity does not mean they will accept cheap offerings that are low-priced owing to subpar performance or inadequate service. As we discuss later in this chapter, they will not usually accept less than parity levels of performance or relational value.

Home furnishing customers in this price value segment are attracted to IKEA and the message of "low price with meaning." Since IKEA does not provide in-store sales assistance, customers have to do everything from taking their own measurements to transporting their purchase home and assembling them. IKEA keeps their total cost below that of competitors with utilitarian designs, and IKEA makes no pretense their products will endure. Nonetheless, IKEA measures up on the basic service features of the retail experience with acceptable quality.

*Relational value.* The decision process for customers in this segment is to first screen the alternatives within their consideration set for acceptable levels of price and performance and then make their choice based on the best service or best total solution. Increasingly, customers are migrating into this segment as the performance and price levels of their choice options are less differentiated (approaching parity).

Edward Jones offers superior relational value, with a personal approach to investing through a local financial advisor. Their target segment is conservative investors uncomfortable with the prospect of making investment decisions without the guidance of a trusted adviser. Their relational value proposition is providing "trusted and convenient face-to-face financial advice to individual investors who delegate their financial decisions." Edward Jones delivers this value proposition with a business model of 18 000 offices in convenient strip malls and retail areas of suburbs, with only one financial advisor per office. An indicator of how well their strategy works is they had the highest investor satisfaction in the 2021 J.D. Power satisfaction survey.

## How do customers choose?

Customer value leaders have deep insights into how and why their customers choose them over other purchase alternatives. If customers see no meaningful differences among these alternatives, they may simply take the best deal, or stick with what they chose previously. There are three guidelines for better understanding how customers make their choices. Strategists ignore them at their peril.

First, they focus on a small subset of all the options. This is termed the "consideration set" or the "evoked set." If a brand is not in this small set, the game is almost over before it begins. Brands are included if they are available, meet a minimal standard of performance or are known (Roberts and Lattin 1991). A useful way to learn about the alternatives in the reduced set is with an unaided awareness question, which simply asks the customer to name all the brands that come to mind in a category.

Second, customers weight the three sources of value differently, and give greater weight to the source of value they prioritize. They do not ignore the other sources, but simply give them less weight in their choice decision. If a brand is judged to be very strong on performance, but is perceived to be terrible on service, the customer may select an alternative with an acceptable level of price and service, even if it is judged slightly lower on performance relative to the strongest alternatives. There is an extensive literature on consumer evaluation processes that can illuminate this question.

Third, customers evaluate offerings relative to a parity (reference) level. Achieving parity is more than just meeting the minimum requirements of the category. Instead, it means at least a moderate, and often a high, level of competence, where customers do not see a meaningful difference among the offerings. Parity is an outside-in concept, as the prospective customer is the arbiter of whether there is meaningful differentiation for their purposes. The issue is not whether there is an actual difference in performance, relational or price value, it is whether customers perceive there is a difference that matters to them. Inside-out firms may deceive themselves that their carefully managed differentiation efforts matter, or are even noticed by their target customers.

The value vectors schematic in Figure 3.2 captures how customers perceive the three basic types of perceived value they consider when making a choice. They will position the choice alternatives as above or below the parity point on each vector, to decide which of the alternatives they are considering given the best weighted combination of the three types of value. This is an insightful schematic for ensuring outside-in thinking pervades a leadership team, since each functional group can quickly grasp the implications.

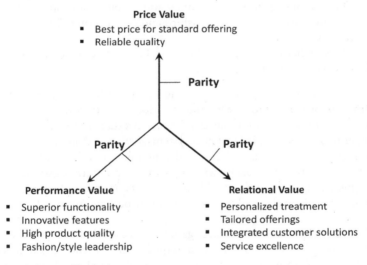

**Price Value**
- Best price for standard offering
- Reliable quality

Parity

Parity

Parity

**Performance Value**
- Superior functionality
- Innovative features
- High product quality
- Fashion/style leadership

**Relational Value**
- Personalized treatment
- Tailored offerings
- Integrated customer solutions
- Service excellence

**Figure 3.2**    The value vectors

We apply these concepts about how customers make their choices, to understand more fully the nature of customer solutions, using the lens of the "mutually determined customer value proposition" perspective (Payne et al. 2017, p. 469).

## Customer solutions as mutually determined CVPs

> "There are products, and there are solutions. A product performs a function. A solution fulfills a human need. People want solutions."
>
> (CEO, 3COM)

Solutions are bundles of products and related services that create value greater than the sum of their parts. To offer a real solution, and not just a repackaging of existing products and services, four criteria should be met:

- Each solution is *co-created* with customers.
- It is therefore *tailored* to each customer.
- The relationship between customer and supplier is unusually *intimate* and involves multiple relationships and connection points across the companies.
- The supplier accepts some of the *risk* through performance-based or risk-based contracts.

As with customer relationship management (CRM) best practices, the aim is to form a one-to-one learning relationship. However, being able to co-create a real solution requires relationships that are much deeper and wider than those enabled by CRM systems, with social and informational connections across many levels and functions of each partner organization. This is most feasible with high-value, long-term customers who are big enough to warrant sizable investments of time and energy by the supplier, and are also willing to make a reciprocal commitment.

Customers who are true partners gain from these relationships in several ways. Overall costs may be lower and quality higher when customers are interacting with a single supplier for multiple activities. They may see benefits from superior performance through preferred access to the latest technology. Their risks may be reduced by sharing them with the supplier.

There are two contrasting ways of thinking about customer solutions, revealed in the research of Tuli et al. (2007). The inside-out view is that "solutions are bundles of products and services that help us sell more" (Tuli et al. 2007, p. 5). The contrasting outside-in view is that, "the purpose of a solution is to help our customers succeed to our mutual benefit" (Tuli et al. 2007, p. 5), by enhancing their performance, decreasing their risks, and reducing their total life cycle costs. How would such a solution appear to a business-to-business (B2B) customer? What factors do they consider in comparing vendors?

*An integrated model of customer solutions: the CVP Octagon.*[2] This portrayal of the dimensions used by B2B customers is adapted from proprietary work for a consortium of companies offering enterprise computer solutions. This eight-factor model for describing, diagnosing, and improving a CVP is portrayed in Figure 3.3.

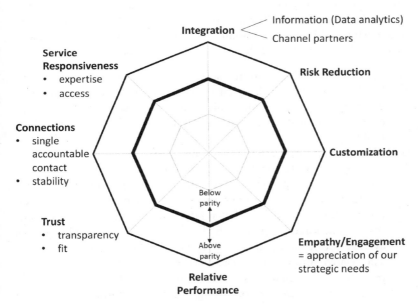

**Figure 3.3**   Diagnosing a customer solution: the CVP octagon

This CVP Octagon shares many features or traits of the Worm et al. (2017) model. According to Worm et al. (2017, p. 501): "The solutions are (1) built on understanding customer requirements, (2) are customized to implement customer activities and/or processes, (3) take the form of an output-based performance contract that delivers on customer-specified metrics, and (4) provide post-deployment support." The CVP Octagon is a more comprehensive portrayal by adding the perceived relative performance of the core offering, perceived empathy (appreciation of the customer's strategic needs), and the integration and analysis of information from the solution. We have subsumed their output-based performance metrics under the broad rubric of risk reduction, which also includes desirable elements, such as "pay for what you use" (as in SaaS offerings). The most notable difference is the inclusion of service responsiveness, the quality and stability of ongoing connections, and perceived trust in the vendor ("do we believe they will do what they promised to do?"). These latter three dimensions of the CVP Octagon are subsumed in the Worm et al. (2017) model as moderators of the link between the solutions offering and profitability growth which was their measure of performance. These differences are attributable to the emphasis of the CVP Octagon on diagnosing and improving a solution versus testing a conceptual model. Some of the key features of this eight-factor diagnostic model are:

- The data are collected from a survey of decision owners (such as the heads of radiology in hospital systems that buy diagnostic imaging equipment). It is important to distinguish these leaders from the influences and implementers, who are also part of the decision-making unit (DMU).
- The survey is administered by a third party that does not reveal the sponsor (to avoid socially desirable response biases).
- Each factor is measured with a series of scale questions about each vendor the respondent knows (provided by an aided recall awareness question), relative to the other vendors in the consideration set. The scale is anchored on parity which is the respondent's judgments of average performance that is neither superior or inferior.
- The relative importance of each factor will vary by market type and probably within market segments. These weights can be measured with an importance scale or through a conjoint analysis.

In common with other conceptual models of customer solutions, the CVP Octagon is a static portrayal. The next chapter provides deeper, systemic understanding of the dynamic forces influencing the ability of customer value leaders to sustain their edge, or for followers and new entrants to get ahead.

## NOTES

1. Portions of this chapter are adapted from Day and Moorman (2010).
2. This section is adapted from Day (2020).

# 4 Sustaining customer value leadership

There is a law in economics that every situation bears the seeds of its own reversal. This is the "law of nemesis" – nothing good lasts indefinitely since others will want to share it. The corollary for customer value leaders is that no competitive advantage is ever secure in the long run, and the definition of the long run is shortening in almost every market. Therefore, the leadership team must have a clear outside-in understanding of the possible scenarios for the evolution of the market it serves, if it is to stay ahead of rivals. There are three main forces shaping the evolution of markets in the current turbulent era: the accelerating pace of market evolution, value priorities are changing, and value leadership is increasingly difficult to sustain.

*Accelerating market evolution.* The product life cycle is the reigning framework for describing how markets are presumed to evolve through the well-known stages of introduction, growth, maturity, and decline. There is a misleading inevitability to this stylized treatment of market evolution that undermines its contribution to strategic thinking. Instead, shrewd strategists understand that each market has its own rhythm, which is shaped by the interactions of customers, competitors, and technologies. These outside-in strategists have better and deeper insights into the following forces.

*Diminishing consumer uncertainty over time.* During the introduction of a new product or category, consumer uncertainty about quality, benefits, and value is at its highest. Some uncertainty occurs since the first offering of a breakthrough product may not be as good as the established products and may be more costly to produce. Over time, customers will gain confidence through experience and information sharing, and the rules of the competitive game – the accepted assumptions about how value is created and captured – will be clearer.

*Coevolution of products and markets.* As markets unfold, their growth potential may be limited by what prospective customers can envision from their experience. This usually underestimates the ultimate potential demand, which emerges only after the market gains experience with the product or service, and innovations improve the performance. The market potential of an emerging technology can be especially difficult to anticipate.

*Morphing market boundaries.* The traditional strategy playbook is anchored on well-defined markets: the competitors are familiar and stable, and the production functions and activities are established and distinct from adjacent categories. As markets evolve and technology advances, firms find themselves in increasingly dynamic and competitive environments. In this new scenario, competition to satisfy customers' requirements comes from unexpected places, especially in the fast-converging computing, social media, financial technologies (fintech), telecommunications, and entertainment industries. Market boundaries have evolved from fixed to fuzzy, with overlapping substitutes and complex role reversals in which business-to-business (B2B) customers may become competitors, and vice versa.

## Changing value priorities: the threat of commoditization

Two processes are especially influential in challenging the established competitive order.

*Customers evolve their criteria.* With experience and repeat purchasing, customers become ever more knowledgeable about the characteristics, appropriate usage patterns, and applications of a product or service. For many customers, the performance value that first attracted their patronage becomes a given, and they may feel less need for technical support and education or quality. These buyers are increasingly confident in their choices and may not believe that there is much difference among the available alternatives.

When this happens, the dominant companies in the market are likely to overshoot the requirements of segments of their target market. In their zeal to keep ahead of their rivals on the performance vector, these companies deliver more functionality and quality than customers in the lower tier of the market can utilize or are willing to pay for. Customers will not keep paying higher prices for benefits that they do not need. This is the essence of Christensen's (2016) theory of disruptive innovation. The basic lessons are still relevant, although the original model was formulated in a hardware industry, which has been supplanted by software, content and services.

*Parity is a moving target.* There is a well-known "herd mentality" among incumbents that leads to continuous jockeying to establish "points of parity" along the value vectors. From toothpaste to orthopedic devices, or 3D printers, the degree of perceived differentiation in performance steadily diminishes because of the relentless process of imitation. Keeping pace with rivals in the served market is a requirement for staying in the game. One effect of everyone keeping pace is that the parity level on each vector steadily moves outward: performance improves, real prices drop, and service becomes better. As parity advances, companies have to spend more just to stay in the game. Customers, especially business customers with dedicated purchasing resources, are more informed and more willing to play one competitor against another. As customers' expectations about acceptable performance on each attribute rise, they are less willing to tolerate below-parity performance on any dimension.

*The broader context of digital turbulence.* The most dynamic and uncertain force shaping the balance of power between buyers and sellers in a relationship, and shifting the competitive arena, will be the unexpected turbulence created by advances in digital technologies. Strategists will struggle to anticipate what may lie ahead when:

- Digital platforms help new global players to emerge in unexpected ways. China now has a large lead in the ability to make mobile payments (roughly 50 times that of the US). In just 15 years, the number of Chinese firms in the Fortune Global 500 has increased by more than 20 times.
- Market boundaries are blurring and dissolving. Fintech is altering the nature of money itself, including how customers transact and secure loans. Big bets are being made by companies on blockchain technologies that enable cryptocurrencies for the decentralized electronic exchange of value.

- Complex ecosystems are emerging. This week's competitor may be next week's supplier, customer, partner, or all of these. While Apple and Samsung compete fiercely in the mobile phone market, Apple relies on Samsung for key components for its phones.
- The pace of change is accelerating. Time is being so compressed that the rate of change is exceeding the ability of traditional, hierarchical organizations to keep up.

Meanwhile, organizations are also grappling with ongoing changes in stakeholder and customer requirements, competitor strategies, access to resources, and the political and regulatory environment. Digital turbulence intensifies all these challenges.

## Defending customer value leadership

The most likely source of an attack on a performance or relational value leader is from the price value vector. This is readily associated with Asian suppliers who emphasize the perceived total cost of the customer value equation, and offer an acceptable level of quality and performance. They seek price-sensitive customers who will not accept cheap offerings that cut costs with substandard quality or inadequate service delivery.

Low-cost, price value rivals can emerge from any direction. European retailers once ignored the threat from the hard-discount rivals Lidl and Aldi, until these discounters unleashed a bare-bones price value attack. This is a story that has been repeated in almost every maturing market, and the same lesson is always learned by the incumbents.

The stakes are especially high for performance value leaders in maturing markets, since the wide diffusion of technology often means that this value vector becomes relatively less important as a differentiator. A strategic move these firms should not make is match the low-cost attacker's prices to drive this rival out of the market. The only sure outcome is that the defender's profit margins will be severely reduced, compromising their ability to compete through innovation. There are three better options for this firm to invest its free cash flow:

1. *Keep innovating.* This option best suits the genetic make-up of a performance leader, and offers the possibility of a game-changing breakthrough that changes the rules of competition. Depending on the type of market these innovations could mean superior design,

a two to five times improvement in performance or a better customer service experience.

2. *Attack the attacker with a low-cost offshoot.* This option is attractive when a newly established and independent operation can share high fixed-cost assets, such as a capital-intensive network or a production system that is dependent on capacity utilization to lower costs.

3. *Emphasize relational value superiority.* This is a compelling option (as we described in the previous chapter) when the largest customer segment prioritizes performance value less than relational value. This is a consequence of the shrinking differences between leaders and average performers as technology diffuses and is copied by all the rivals. This has occurred with digital technologies.

A common pattern of evolution in the growing importance of the relational value vector is shown in Figure 4.1. The length of each value vector is proportional to the size of the segment that gives most importance to the attributes of the vector. As the market matures, both the price and relational value vectors become larger (while parity continues to move out along each vector):

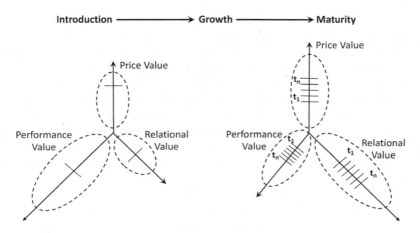

**Figure 4.1**    Evolving value segments

Shifting to a relational value positioning based on becoming a solution provider is challenging for most companies. Some in the leadership team will question whether the advantages will offset the greater risk exposure and customer dependency. These downsides were revealed during the demand shocks of the pandemic. Whereas an integrated solutions strategy might have helped customers recover quickly, in practice they were rendered ineffective and the providers absorbed most of the risks. Selling a service on subscription or usage pricing is a profitless sinkhole when factories are closed and supply chains are compromised and slow. These setbacks are unlikely to slow the move to relational value strategies being driven by larger trends, such as cloud platforms providing comprehensive solutions services across the globe.

## Integrating outside-in and inside-out considerations

One of the guiding premises shaping marketing strategies is that strategy making should start with a wide-angled, outside-in view, and then iterate to consider inside-out constraints, resources and capabilities. We delve deeply into this process in Chapter 8, but begin here with a tool named the value stick and introduce the business model that a firm uses to create and capture the customer value.

This framework answers an outside-in question ("How much are customers willing to pay?"), and an inside-out question ("What is the minimum we are willing to accept?") The difference between the customer's willingness to pay (WTP) and the company's willingness to sell (WTS) is the value a firm is said to create (Brandenburger and Stuart 1996; Oberholzer-Gee 2020). Within this stripped-down framework there are only two ways to create more value; increase WTP or lower WTS. By simplifying strategy to this degree, the proponents believe that strategic thinking is improved and outcomes are better. No evidence is supplied for these assertions.

A successful strategy move, by value-stick standards, either raises the customer's WTP by innovating the offering, or creates value for suppliers by lowering their operating costs or increasing productivity. Both WTP and WTS are evaluated relative to the firm's price and cost, as shown in Figure 4.2.

The value stick is a useful tool for creatively analyzing a case study in a classroom, but overlooks most of the complexities of customer value

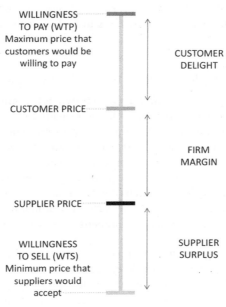

**Figure 4.2** The value stick

creation by not considering perceived risk, market segmentation differences, and the multistage choice process that compares suppliers. The difficulties of measuring these constructs is either ignored or brushed aside.

The proponents readily concede that the concepts of WTP and WTS are abstract, so they mostly revert to using a venerable visualization tool known as the "value map" to reveal market realities. A value map displays the product and service attributes used by a customer segment to: (1) evaluate the offerings in a competitive set – not necessarily the consideration set; (2) rank the attributes by their importance to customers; and (3) link those attributes judged to be most important to the business model and key performance indicators (KPIs). The rankings by managers should be contrasted with the insights from choice models or trade-off/conjoint analyses. The value map can reveal opportunities to innovate with new ways to satisfy customers and differentiate the value proposition. We discuss this innovation path in more detail in the next chapter.

This is an overly simple way to incorporate inside-out considerations into strategy making. A better approach is to look directly into the business model.

## The business model: creating and capturing customer value

If the value proposition is *what* the firm provides the target segment, then the business model is *how* this value is provided profitably. The word "model" can connote a complex and abstract representation. Good business models are anything but abstract. They answer two enduring sets of questions. (1) What business activities are needed to create the customer value? How are these activities sequenced or connected to each other? Who carries out each of these activities? and (2) How do we capture some of the value we create in order to sustain profitability and continually reinvest in innovation to sustain competitive leadership?

*The value-creating system.* This is the system of activities that a business links together to create and deliver customer value, from acquiring the basic inputs and services, to the channel activities required to sell, service, and distribute an offering. These activities coalesce around capabilities (such as order fulfilment, software design and integrity testing, or service delivery), becoming complex bundles of skills, knowledge and system, exercised through distinct processes that sequence the activities. There are only a few distinctive capabilities or core competencies of a business that really contribute to the creation of superior customer value.

Successful business models reinforce and complement the strategic choices of segment target and value proposition. When Dow Corning, the global leader in silicone-based products, faced a challenge to their relational value strategy of providing high-touch design services, personalized sales support, and a great deal of flexibility in terms and conditions, they reinvented their business model. The trigger was a growing segment of price-sensitive, volume buyers that was asking for the same high quality of resins, but at a lower price for high volume, standardized products, such as bathtub calking materials that did not require a high-touch service model. This threatened to open the market to low-cost, offshore competitors.

To prevail in the emerging low-end, standardized market segment, the company created a separate low-cost business model within a new organization named Xiameter. Sales and distribution costs were slashed by eliminating technical service activities, lengthening order lead times, and limiting order-size flexibility. The company also benefited from a scalable online ordering and fulfilment system, with all communications solely by email.

*The value-capturing system.* The ultimate business model question is, "How does the company get paid for the value it creates?" There have been many dramatic changes over the past few decades, and for many companies these changes have been involuntary. The media industry, in general, has struggled with this aspect of their business model in an era of easy downloads and file sharing.

The most common form of innovation in value capture has been the shift from a product-sale model to a service model. Today, you can lease industrial carpet as readily as a copier. To complete the system and highlight the integration of the business model with the value proposition, recall that when the customer pays for performance, or pays for what they use, it also reduces their perceived risk.

## Summary

Customer value leaders create superior value that their target customers will pay for, by formulating an integrated strategy from the outside in. This strategy answers two big questions. The first is, "what needs of which market segments are we going to serve better than anyone else, while being seen as competent and competitive in meeting the rest of this segment's needs?" This choice provides a positioning theme around which an organization can mobilize its resources and capabilities. The second question is about the business model that consistently delivers and captures the value, "What activities are needed to create the value we promise our target customers and how do we make money?"

The leadership team must have a well-informed view of how their target segments will evolve, and how they should adapt to these dynamic forces that create new opportunities and threats. This is a never-ending task. Customer value leaders are realists; they realize they can never underestimate any current or emerging competitors, or fall behind in responding to the shifts and changes in technology and customer requirements. It takes the sustained innovation discussed in the next two chapters, to keep both the value proposition and business model fresh and viable.

# 5 Innovating new value for customers: the full-spectrum approach

For all the veneration of innovators in the media, few firms have demonstrated a sustained ability to grow faster organically by innovating with their own resources. However, these firms exist, and prosper. Growth leaders as diverse as 3M, Airbnb, Starbucks, Amazon, LEGO and Sephora consistently outperform their rivals by better executing their outside-in and inside-out approaches to innovation. This chapter addresses two principal reasons for their resilient and sustained approach to innovation.

First, customer value innovators have a more expansive approach to innovation. They consider the full spectrum of possibilities for growth; by reimagining and stretching every dimension of their strategy. They surmount the constraints of inside-out innovation that emphasizes improving features and functions, by deeply understanding and then anticipating the changing needs of their current and prospective markets.

Second, these growth leaders nurture a supportive climate for continuous innovation, and promote a growth-enabling innovation narrative (Day and Shea 2020). This climate is shaped by an externally orientated culture, unwavering leadership support, adequate resources, and the right metrics and rewards. Innovation cultures are based on trust; people throughout the organization feel their ideas are valued and it is safe to pursue them. These cultures flourish when the leadership team is fully immersed in the execution of the growth strategy. This does not mean micro-managing projects; instead, it requires active surveillance and interventions when needed, while giving people permission to take "well-intended risks," to borrow a term that pervades the innovation dialogue within the 3M Company.

## Full-spectrum innovation

Few firms lack ideas to pursue. A reactive approach will sweep up a lot of possibilities: research and development (R&D) will envision new features and performance enhancements; distributors, salespeople, and employees will suggest new services; there will be pressure to match or leapfrog a competitor by copying and adapting their innovations; and changes in strategy will require (and inspire) supporting innovations. While these sources of ideas should always be encouraged, the chances of coming up with a breakthrough idea by waiting and reacting are much lower than if there is a directed search.

A directed search for opportunities, will surface better quality ideas sooner than simply waiting for these opportunities to emerge. If the competitors exploits an idea sooner, it is much harder to gain an advantage. The benefits will be further lessened if the search is confined to familiar places, where most of the development activity has been focused in the past. To combat the narrowing forces of habit, the full-spectrum innovation approach proposes 12 growth pathways.

The basis of the full-spectrum approach to identifying and pursuing innovation opportunities is the questioning, challenging and reimagining of each dimension of the strategy formulated in Chapters 3 and 4. The departure point is challenging the *customer value proposition*, by posing these guiding questions:

- *Customers:* what other needs of our current customers can we serve? What other customers could we serve? How can we keep more of them?
- *Offerings:* how and where can we leverage our capabilities and brand and apply emerging technology possibilities? How can we change the competitive game, and preempt current and possible rivals?

Applying the same logic to probe the business model, the guiding questions are:

- *Value creating:* what business activities are needed to create the value we promise our present and prospective customers?
- *Value capturing:* how can we make sufficient money while creating value for our customers?

Asking and answering these questions generates many growth pathways. Our full-spectrum approach to identifying the 12 potential pathways builds on other approaches[1] while applying recent advances in design thinking, open innovation, dynamic capabilities, the contributing of ecosystems, and business model innovation. Our emphasis is on innovations that will drive superior organic growth. These growth pathways are consistent with higher-level typology (Satell 2017) that distinguishes four types of innovation by asking two questions: how well can we define the problem (that innovation is to solve) and how well can we define the skill domain(s) needed to solve it? Depending on how these two questions are answered, an innovation could be (1) sustaining, (2) disruptive, (3) breakthrough or (4) basic research. In my experience, the growth pathways approach best balances approaches that provide narrow guidance on how to find opportunities, versus offering broad prescriptions that lack specificity.

## Pathways to faster growth

The full-spectrum innovation coin has two sides. On one side is the customer value proposition with eight possible pathways to follow; on the other side are the four business model pathways that spell out how the business can profitably fulfill the promise of the value proposition innovations. As Figure 5.1 shows, growth pathways can start on either side, but success requires the two sides to be tightly linked and synchronized.

Each growth pathway can be combined with other pathways, in myriad ways. The reach and ambition of the innovation along each pathway can range from small-*i* thinking to BIG-*I* breakthroughs. The variety of possible combinations can be daunting, but also encouraging. Equity markets reward a value-adding variety of growth initiatives – offering grounds for optimism for any firm whose growth is lagging. It is unlikely that all the best combinations have been explored and exploited. The challenge is not a lack of attractive pathways, but finding the energy and imagination to systematically pursue them ahead of rivals. In the rest of this chapter we dissect each pathway and show how growth leaders use them to generate innovations that drive growth.

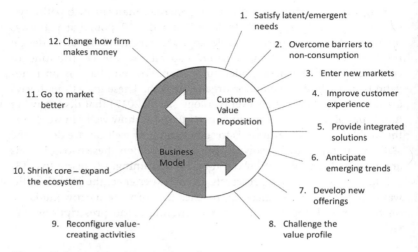

**Figure 5.1**    The 12 growth pathways

## Pathway 1: satisfy latent or emergent needs

The global pandemic jump-started or accelerated many trends, and few were as consequential as the shift to remote working. With the aid of faster broadband and Zoom, Slack and other collaborative platforms, most companies were expected to downsize their offices. What does this mean for the layout of these offices? The office furniture maker Herman Miller drew on their deep insights into office design and anticipated that employees would need to have more autonomy to shape their own work-place. The company created a clever "un-system" of furniture that can be moved easily on demand – pushed into groups or pulled away for solo work – without getting approval or needing help.

The Herman Miller approach exemplifies a robust outside-in innovation process applied by firms such as IDEO to develop new offerings in response to a growth challenge (see Figure 5.2).

There are many variants of this process (Brown 2008; Martin 2009a), as we saw in Chapter 2, but each gives a central role to observational or ethnographic methods. The core idea is that latent needs are "evident but not yet obvious." They require skilled observers who can immerse themselves in the target customer's world. Many other tools can be

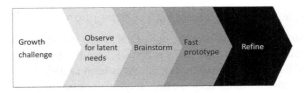

**Figure 5.2**      The design thinking process

used to extract deep customer insights with a directed search, including in-depth interviews, structured listening, problem identification, and metaphor-elicitation methods. In order to better hear the voice of the customer, firms can also try these methods:

- *Leverage lead users.* These are users who face needs in advance of the rest of the market, and are working to find a solution sooner. Products such as correction fluid, sports bras, and Gatorade came from lead users (professional typists and elite athletes, respectively). In categories such as construction equipment or scientific test instruments, most innovation ideas come from alterations to products or workarounds made by lead users (Urban and von Hippel 1986).
- *Monitor complainers and defectors.* Myopia about customers can be combated by learning from unhappy customers, who express frustration when their needs are not met or understood.
- *Hunt for precursors in the parts of the country or globe where fads, fashions, or technology innovations tend to appear earlier.* Companies such as the footwear-maker Converse have used "cool hunters" and trend trackers as an early warning radar, to uncover trends, such as the rise of retro in clothing and shoes.

Lead user analysis is especially effective at capturing rich information about emerging needs. Another approach yielding complementary insights into underserved needs is the "elements of value" model (Almquist et al. 2016). There are 30 elements of value, ranging from reduces risk, connects, and informs, to self-actualization, that address four types of needs: functional, emotional, life changing, and social impact. In general, the more elements of value provided by a brand, the greater the customer's loyalty and the higher the firm's sustained top-line growth rate.

## Pathway 2: overcome barriers to consumption

Non-customers come in many guises. One group is close to the currently served market. They occasionally may purchase the industry's offerings, but could become enthusiastic customers as soon as they discover a superior alternative. Perhaps they are only buying because they have to – think of health insurance, or taxi cab users before Uber.

The key to satisfying these non-consumers is by deeply understanding the value they are seeking and their pain points. The fast-food chain Pret A Manger succeeded by doing just that. They offered restaurant-quality sandwiches made fresh daily, using superior ingredients and ready to grab and go. By satisfying this group with a superior alternative, they attracted more customers like them.

A more difficult group of non-consumers to satisfy, are not necessarily uninterested but face barriers. Four barriers have been identified (Anthony et al. 2008):

1. *Lack of money*. Existing alternatives are too expensive.
2. *Lack of skills*. Existing alternatives are complex, requiring expert guidance or a large amount of training.
3. *Lack of access*. Alternatives can be consumed only in specific contexts, locations, and so on.
4. *Lack of time*. Consumption of alternatives takes too long.

Microfinance overcame these barriers by offering microloans to disadvantaged entrepreneurs who lacked access to banks or credit facilities. This expanded the lending industry to lift people out of poverty. The Nintendo Wii home video game console, overcame the money and skills barriers by offering an intuitive product that even non-gamers could immediately enjoy, at a significant discount (about 30 percent) to other gaming platforms.

## Pathway 3: enter or develop emerging segments' sub-categories or geographies

This growth pathway is a set of linked hiking routes starting from the same trail-head. Successfully traversing each trail demands a deep outside-in immersion into the differences among (1) the benefits sought by present and prospective customers, (2) the intensity of competitive rivalry in the prospective segment or geography, (3) the availability of channel intermediaries, and (4) the capabilities and financial resources available.

*Customer segment growth opportunities.* There is a potential trap here: customers can only sort themselves into benefit or choice segments by responding to what is on offer in the product category. These are the "what is" segments in contrast with the "might be" segments formed by overcoming the trade-offs and compromises some customers have to make. This creative rethinking could be a pathway to the creation of a new sub-category (Aaker 2020). In 2008, Warby-Parker challenged the established retail market for eyewear with an online channel that created a new customer segment and sub-category. Their prices were 75 percent below those charged by optometrists, to keep them affordable. To solve the problem of getting the right fit when trying on eyewear was not possible, they sent out five frames with glasses to be returned within five days at no charge.

*What prospects in new geographies?* Until recently this was an attractive pathway, fueled by a steady advance in globalization (owing to the increasing interconnectedness of the world economy). This interdependence of geographies and countries has continued to increase, but has been slowed sharply by the forces of nationalism and protectionism, abetted by the populism that led to Brexit. Looking ahead, the most likely outcome is the evolution of the global economy into regional trading blocs (Krueger 2020) and fewer degrees of freedom to grow.

Meanwhile, the presumption that innovations developed for the demanding markets of the US, Europe, and Japan will, with some adaptation, also meet the needs of rapidly developing countries, has been challenged on two fronts. First, stripped-down versions are not enough; consumers in developing countries respond when offerings meet their unique needs. Second, innovations focused on developing-market customers are increasingly proving to be appealing to developed-country consumers interested in simplicity, ease of use, or energy efficiency. The traditional flow of innovation from rich to poor countries may move in reverse (Govindarayan and Trimble 2012).

### Pathway 4: improve the customer experience across all touch points

Every purchase decision by a customer, from installing a medical device to choosing and staying at a hotel, has a distinct beginning, middle, and end, with many steps along the way that take place over time. The key to this pathway is to first capture the complete customer experience from the customer's perspective, not what you hoped or expected the customer to experience. There are many ways to map the customer experience or journey (for example, Kalbach 2021); I prefer approaches that also capture the emotional state of the customer during their journey. Are they feeling "great," "neutral," or "upset" at each step.

Once the steps are sequenced, new customer value can be created by asking which steps in the process could be opportunities for improvement:

- Which steps can be improved? Westin Hotels created the "Heavenly Experience" after interviews and observations of people getting ready for bed revealed the importance that business travelers gave to a good night's sleep.
- Which steps can be eliminated, combined in a different sequence, or made smarter? Can the burden be automated, or shifted elsewhere?
- Where are the pain points?
- What factors dictate who gets included in the consideration set?
- Where can time delays be eliminated?

With an outside-in view of what the customer sees, hears, feels, and does, companies can improve their existing offering or find white space (unspoken, unmet needs of customers) opportunities. The key is to rethink all points of contacts, even the prosaic ones.

The upending of the customer experience with frozen yogurt in 2010 displayed these possibilities for innovation on this pathway. When "The Country's Best Yogurt" (TCBY) was in ascendance, the customer went to a counter and a server assembled a yogurt cup using pre-measured portions and charging for each topping. In the early 2000s TCBY had nearly 1800 stores. By 2021 they were reduced to 300 struggling stores – replaced by a customer self-service model started by Pinkberry. The customer first chooses and pours the flavor of yogurt they prefer into a cup, then decides how much of each topping to add, and pays by total weight at the checkout counter. The lesson here is that customers really want to be in control of their purchase journey. An obvious point, perhaps, with powerful implications.

## Pathway 5: provide integrated customer solutions

In Chapter 3 we developed four criteria to be met if a solution is creating value for customers that is more than the sum of its parts:

1. It is co-created with customers.
2. It is tailored to each customer's requirements.
3. It delivers superior service on the customer's terms, including rapid response, ready access, and clear accountability from the supplier.
4. Some of the risk perceived by customers is absorbed by suppliers through performance- or risk-based contracts or commitments.

It is facile to label a bundle that enables one-stop shopping as a "solution." However, these are not valuable innovations. Competitors can copy them easily, and so they do not typically result in growth. Growth comes from solutions based on outside-in insights into how to solve a customer's problems.

The British cyber security firm Sophos saw that most of their customers were struggling to coordinate security across multiple end-points (Raptine, mobile phone, tablet, IOS software, Android software, and so on) when the rules were constantly changing. These firms lacked the deep knowledge of the incessant cyber threats from hacking, or how to maintain a secure network across diverse end-points. To meet this pressing need Sophos created industry-targeted sets of components that secured both networks and devices. They were easier to deploy because they were designed to work together. With a cost-effective and simpler solution, Sophos was able to serve the medium to small enterprise companies that could not afford the complex solutions. They have even released a home version, to bring integrated security to individuals.

## Pathway 6: anticipate emerging trends and issues

Fedex found great opportunities in global components handling enabled by trends in globalized freight flows, outsourcing demands, and Internet availability. Trends often emerge from fringe markets and extend outward. This is how snowboarding, microbrewers, and extreme sports became popular with mainstream markets.

These are industry-specific trends to be foreseen and monitored as a source of opportunities and threats (Day and Schoemaker 2019). Other possibilities will emerge with a wider lens. While, many companies are developing sustainability strategies and adopting more sustainable practices, this may be a precursor to bigger changes in how businesses operate. From clean technology (cleantech), to the circular economy, sustainability is taking a broader meaning, ESG (environmental, social, and governance) criteria are shaping investment choices, and companies are looking for help in meeting their obligations. These shifts will surely rearrange the innovation landscape.

*Innovating the offering.* A superior capability for anticipation is an essential ingredient for success when innovating the offering aspect of the customer value proposition. The first six pathways are about an outside-in approach to customer opportunities, the next two pathways open the outside-in lens wider to consider technological advances and the moves and counter moves of competitors.

Vanguard the nonprofit investment giant, was an early adopter of artificial intelligence to bring financial guidance to its customers at a lower cost. Its Personal Advisor Service systems automates tasks, such as rebalancing a portfolio toward a target mix, or providing goals-based forecasts in real time, while human advisers take on higher-value activities and serve as "investing coaches." The payoff has been maintaining lower costs while keeping customer satisfaction high.

## Pathway 7: develop innovative new products, services, or platforms

This pathway is more like an autobahn or expressway for most companies; it is a wide pathway that absorbs the most resources. It is generally the best managed of the innovation activities, with well-honed guidance from tools, such as stage-gating, and real-options investments. The focus is on the application of new knowledge and technology developments, put in new combinations that add value to customers. (For example, think of the Global Positioning System, GPS, or antilock braking systems, ABS.) This pathway is most productive when it is guided by deep insights into latent or unsatisfied needs.

The technology base for this pathway can be either sustaining or disruptive to the business. A *disruptive* technology has the potential to invalidate existing advantages, and is hard for an incumbent to match as it would compromise existing resources. This is especially a risk when the established technology is complex and costly, relative to a disruptive technology that is cheaper and simpler while good enough to meet the needs of most customers. This is how Salesforce.com disrupted the market for customer relationship management (CRM) software. The incumbents, such as SAP, sold high-priced enterprise software customized to each customer, and charged high fees for installation. Instead, Salesforce.com sold software as a service, and rented access to their programs in the "cloud." These programs were easy to use and significantly cheaper than the incumbents' offering, which suited most medium-size and small customers. While disruptive technologies receive a lot of attention – they challenge the status quo – most technology advances are of the sustaining variety; incumbents can adopt them without undercutting their value proposition.

Two important variants on this growth pathway are design and platform innovations. A platform could be a set of modular components that serve as the building blocks of a family of products or services. With these modules, a diverse set of offerings can be created more rapidly and cheaply than by designing each offering separately. Other general platforms such as the AI assistants Amazon Echo/Alexa or Google Home/Assistant are vehicles for innovation (Dawar and Bendle 2018). These platforms provide detailed information on consumer behavior and motivations, enabling companies to rethink their products and marketing approaches to better meet consumers' needs and sharpen their differentiation. They will be better able to detect and respond to rapid or subtle shifts in consumer requirements.

Design innovation seeks to create products with appearance and functionality that make them instantly recognizable. The emphasis here is on creativity, often expressed through high-quality and artistic form factors. This is at the heart of Bang & Olufsen (B&O), the Danish maker of televisions, sound systems, telephones, and other electronic devices. New ideas, materials, and technologies made their way into B&O products when designers put them there, and engineers then had to find ways to make them at scale.

*A false dichotomy.* One trap to avoid is to treat demand-pull approaches (finding customers' needs and solving them) and supply-push approaches (developing a technology then finding or creating a market for it) as alternative or strategic choices to be made (Pisano 2015). This has overtones of the false dichotomy of inside-out or outside-in. They are not choices, but iterative approaches that must be integrated.

This integrated approach helps explain how James Dyson transformed vacuum cleaners. Consumers had every right to be frustrated with the way their upright units quickly lost suction because the disposable bags became clogged with dirt particles. This was an obvious design flaw, and yet vacuum cleaners had been made that way for a century. After a great deal of experimentation, Dyson found the solution in a novel design that used powerful centrifugal force to separate the dirt from the air. While this may seem like an idea that should have been implemented decades earlier, it was enabled by advances in the formulation and performance of polycarbonate plastics.

*Innovative imitation.* Imitations often can become winners, but they have to do more than just copy. The key is to understand the appeal of the original innovation, and the barriers to its success, with an eye to making improvements in ways that customers will value. Thus, the iPod was not the first digital music player, and the iPhone was not the first smartphone. Apple took the originators' concepts and made them far more appealing and usable. The multibillion-dollar category of own-label, or private label, products is based on copying well-known brands but at a much lower price point for the same quality. Fast-fashion firms such as ZARA have prospered by copying designs from the catwalk and getting them on to hangers in retail stores far faster than competitors (or even the original designers).

Followers usually have lower R&D costs, and face less risk of failure since the product concept has already been market tested. To win, they need to learn from the pioneer's problems and deploy an agile organization that can move quickly to develop a better version before other competitors are tempted to follow. Another way for an innovative imitator to win is to unleash a much larger go-to-market capability and cover the market more thoroughly.

## Pathway 8: challenge the value map

This pathway gained traction with the popularity of "blue ocean strategy" (Kim and Manborgne 2014). The message is that sustained growth is best achieved by creating new markets. This approach goes beyond growth pathway 3, to emphasize finding untapped market spaces and creating new demand. Paragons of this approach are Airbnb, Uber and Curves Fitness Centers. Within the "red oceans" of established markets – tinted red with the blood of rivals fighting for advantage within a fixed opportunity – there is arguably less potential for growth. This is an appealing notion, with the caveat that little is known about the risks of creating new markets versus the rewards, nor are there stories of firms that tried to follow the guidance and failed.

To find a potential "blue ocean," start with a value profile of the varying levels of product or service features offered by the current players, and challenge this profile with these questions:

1. Which of the features the industry takes for granted can be eliminated?
2. Which features could be reduced well below industry standards?
3. Which features could be raised above industry standard?
4. Which features could be created that have never been offered?

The value profile should include all the features beyond the core offering that customers use when making a choice. The basis of the approach is creatively challenging industry conventional wisdom and works best in tandem with other growth pathways.

This was the approach used to design the Ginger budget hotel chain, launched in India by the Tata Group. The chain was designed to meet the needs of frequent business travelers who wanted a place to stay that was not as earthy or as unpredictable as a low-price hotel, but who would not pay the prices of a 5-star hotel. The Ginger brand promises a customer experience that is "consistent, simple, light-hearted" at the best price. The small rooms are strictly no-frills, with dorm-style furniture, but with state-of-the-art new mattresses. Costs are tightly controlled by locating the hotels in business districts, away from high-cost real estate, and using self-check-in and minimal staff. The resulting competitive profile (shown in Figure 5.3) clearly sets Ginger apart from the competing hotels and aligns the hotel with the needs of its target segment.

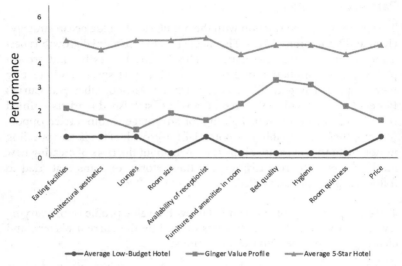

**Source:** Published materials, site visits, and hotel reviews.

**Figure 5.3**    Innovating the budget hotel market in India

## Summary: outside-in innovation

We introduced the full-spectrum approach to innovation, achieved by stretching and reimagining every dimension of the strategy. This yields a total of 12 growth pathways that can be pursued in a myriad of combinations, and with varying degrees of ambition (from modestly incremental to highly disruptive). The aim is to innovate to accelerate organic growth. The customer value proposition can be innovated along eight pathways; each is best approached from the outside in. In the next chapter we treat the business model in the same way, but start the innovation process from the inside out.

# NOTE

1.  For other ways of specifying innovation pathways see Sawhney et al. (2006), Moore (2005), McGrath and MacMillan (2005) and Keeley et al. (2013).

# 6     Innovating the business model

The four pathways for innovating the business model complete the full-spectrum approach to accelerating organic growth.[1] These pathways start from the inside out with four questions about the system for *creating and delivering* customer value, and *capturing* some of that value for the firm (Osterwalder and Pigneau 2010; Birkinshaw and Ansari 2015): (1) what activities need to be carried out? (2) How should these activities be sequenced and connected (Porter and Siggelkow 2008)? (3) Who carries out each activity? (4) How will the value be captured?

Peter Drucker (1994) held an expansive view of a firm's business model, which he named "The theory of the business" and had three parts: assumptions about the environment, the mission, and the competencies and activities needed to accomplish this mission. Together these three assumptions define what an organization gets paid for, what results it wants, and what it must excel at in order to sustain its competitive position.

A business model is a purposeful weaving together of interdependent activities. Some activities will be performed by the firm and others by suppliers, partners or customers (Zott and Amit 2009). They can be combined in a myriad of ways to create a rich set of possibilities. Let us look at the strategic choices made by a start-up with a breakthrough in friction-reduction technology that could be applied to any product with moving parts. Once a target customer segment, such as automobiles, was targeted as the best opportunity, many hard choices still had to be made. Should they build machines that embedded and exploited the technology? Operate a job-shop to perform surface treatment for partners? License the technology to third parties, such as machine tool makers? Each option required developing a different set of capabilities, within the firm or beyond it, and set the prices, operating margins, risk exposure and profit potential. Once a choice of business model is made it is hard to reverse, and certainly limits the array of future strategic moves.

## Pathway 9: reconfigure value-creating activities

The Zara apparel chain, pioneer of the fast-fashion concept, totally rethought its design and manufacturing processes. At most clothing makers the value-creation process starts with designers, who plan collections as much as a year in advance, and it requires long lead times and manufacturing in Asia in order to contain costs. At Zara, fashion and sales trends are monitored continuously to guide their in-house designers, who then fashion what is currently popular. These designs are sent to company-owned factories in Spain, where just-in-time systems can move a blouse, dress, or coat from the drawing board to a store in less than a month. Since Zara is more attuned to the latest fashion, it can change more often and does not have to mark down large inventories of unsold items at the end of each season. This success story suggests two ways of thinking about this pathway: treating business model innovation as a dynamic capability, and adopting advances in technology.

*Manage as a dynamic capability* (Teece 2018). Previously, we saw the benefits of superior sensing, seizing, and transforming dynamic capabilities in keeping a strategy (and the enabling business model) aligned with the changes in the market. Firms with strong dynamic capabilities have greater flexibility in making shifts in resources or activities. This puts a premium on well-honed vigilance capabilities to sense and explore subtle signals of emerging trends.

*Apply advances in technology.* Most business model innovations are prompted and enabled by emerging technologies, especially those underpinning digital transformations that make it possible to combine and coordinate activities and provide new functions. For example, platform business models, such as the ride-sharing app pioneered by Uber, improve the rider experience by quickly integrating the activities and requests of thousands of drivers and riders.

It is not easy to get the timing of the technology right. Being too early alerts rivals to the possibilities while the pioneer absorbs most of the risk of market development. This explains why the shipping giant, Maersk Line, took 20 years before adopting containerization. They waited for standards to be set and for the technology to mature, then moved decisively by building larger ships and modern port facilities (Pedersen Sornn-Friese 2015).

Also, align the business model to segment realities. When Dow Corning, the global leader in silicone-based products, faced a significant threat to its relational value strategy of providing high-end design services, personalized sales support, and flexibility to its buyers, they bifurcated their business model. Price-sensitive buyers were asking for high quality, reliability, and lower prices for the standardized items they were buying. This opened the market to low-cost offshore competitors.

To protect their position at the price-sensitive end of the market, the company built a low-cost business model tailored to the needs of this segment, within a new and very lean organization called XIAMETER. Sales and distribution costs were slashed by eliminating technical service, lengthening lead times from hours to days, and limiting order-size flexibility and custom handling. The new company used only an online ordering system, and all communication was solely by e-mail. Meanwhile their high-touch model still appealed to the other 70 percent of the market.

## Pathway 10: shrink the core–expand the ecosystem (Gulati 2009)

This pathway is started by deciding which activities need to be held by the firm, and which can be outsourced, while ensuring that bottleneck assets are closely controlled. One benefit of working with external suppliers is that scarce resources and leadership attention are freed up for more innovative activities. This is why so many firms have shifted to cloud computing providers for non-critical information technology activities. Bharti Airtel became the second largest mobile phone company in the world by limiting their core activities to customer care, marketing, finance, and the regulatory interface, while outsourcing all the rest of the activities, including providing and maintaining all their equipment.

Also, along this pathway is the practice of open innovation (Chesborough 2003; Rogers et al. 2019). This is a distributed innovation process that purposively manages knowledge flows across the boundaries of the firm. The choice to be open is not simply a matter of bolting on a few R&D partners, taking stakes in early-stage companies, or posting a prize on the Internet. Open innovation takes a change in mind-set to give up some of the control that comes with ownership. While you must cede some ownership, a partner outside the bounds of the firm still has to be closely coordinated.

The shift from closed to open innovation was accelerated by the success of Proctor & Gamble's (P&G's) "connect and develop" model (Huston and Sakkab 2006). This was an explicit recognition that for every P&G researcher, there were 200 scientists or engineers who were just as good in their areas, and that, historically, many of P&G's best ideas had come from teams working across division boundaries. Top management support for this move was crucial, capped by CEO A.G. Lafley, who set a goal that half the company's future new products would come from partners.

## Pathway 11: enhance the go-to-market approach

The convention in business model thinking that distinguishes value creation (pathways 9 and 10) from value delivery (this pathway) is misleading. The go-to-market approach should contribute considerable customer value. The sales team provides useful information, diagnoses problems, and works with the customer to create an integrated solution (pathway 5). The delivery component of the business model includes the supply chain, but goes further to include the chain of value-adding activities in the go-to-market system shown in Figure 6.1.

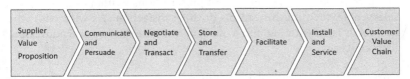

**Figure 6.1**    Activities of intermediaries

This pathway begins with communication and persuasion. In 2012 (Cendrowski 2012, p. 83) Nike's CEO presciently observed that "Connecting [with customers] used to be, 'Here's some product and here's some advertising; we hope you like it' ... Connecting today is a dialogue." This view explains Nike's shift in its marketing efforts. Nike's money has been shifting to online activities and social media, and to supporting communities of users with common interests, since 2011 – well ahead of others. Some of this helps insulate Nike from celebrity endorsements that have gone wrong, which have become so common to our era. However, it also delivers meaningful customer value by improving the customer's (whether a runner, basketball player, or couch potato) experience, and keeps Nike ahead of rivals.

There is potential for growth-enhancing innovation in every activity a firm takes to reach, persuade, and fulfill customer requirements. Some of these innovations respond to the growing complexity of customer solutions and the need to rethink the role of the traditional sales force in an era of ubiquitous access to detailed information. This rethink was accelerated during the pandemic, with B2B customers switching to online methods for searching, talking with suppliers and transacting routine orders. Other innovations respond to cost pressures, more demanding and connected customers, and global competition.

In the pharmaceutical industry, the traditional model had armies of sales representatives fanning out to "detail" doctors, armed with tightly scripted sales pitches on a specific (patent-protected) drug. Multiple sales representatives from the same company might call on the same doctor. But doctors now have less time, and even less patience, for these sales pitches. In response, some firms are asking their representatives to act more like resources for doctors and medical practices. This requires innovations in how drug representatives are motivated and evaluated; one firm no longer uses number of prescriptions written as a metric for salespeople, focusing instead on doctor satisfaction. As with Nike, the new focus is on entering into a dialogue with the doctors and addressing their concerns.

Currently, the most popular word in retail and consumer goods markets is "omnichannel," which is the seamless integration of online and offline shopping activities (Gallino and Rooderkerk 2020). These interconnected channels span the physical and digital environments, include channels that are not controlled by the firm, and require seamless integration. New technologies, such as Alibaba's cloud shelf and interactive fitting room, are further blurring the line between online and offline. These shifts, plus the ability of consumer goods companies to access customer journey data and understand consumer choices better, open up a myriad of opportunities for innovation.

## Pathway 12: change how the firm makes money

The ultimate business model question is "How will the firm capture some of the value it provides to customers?" That is, "How does the company get paid for the value it creates?" There have been drastic changes in many industries over the past few decades in answer to this question. For some firms, these changes have been involuntary. The media industry has struggled to innovate how firms make money in an era of easy downloads and file sharing. While many customers are abandoning the traditional cable package, neither the firms that produce entertainment (such as HBO) or the firms that deliver it (such as Comcast) have been able to innovate an à la carte approach, which customers clearly want, while making enough money to sustain themselves.

The most dramatic innovation of the value-capture system is the shift from a product-sale model to a service model. Now you can lease industrial carpet as easily as a copier. Service models are not just about leasing. Praxair captures the increased value of delivering gases to the point of use in a factory instead of just dropping off a tank car. Castrol Industrial innovated a model to share gains from reducing use of its products based on advice it gave to a client; the firm now captures increased value by advising its customers on how to buy *less* product. The pandemic accelerated the "Xaas" model, of converting everything including software, to a service that can be delivered online. We saw in Chapter 2 that customers want their suppliers to absorb some or all their risks. The Israeli firm Netafirm, a market leader in drip-irrigation systems, faced great difficulty in persuading smaller farmers to engage with and pay for their expensive system. Netafirm overcame this resistance by offering farmers a free installed system with periodic maintenance, to be paid for with a share of each farmer's increased crop yields. They could afford to do this because the risks for the firm could be managed with their deeper knowledge and ability to spread the risk. If the system should fail at one farm, Netafirm could make up for it elsewhere.

# Which way to grow?

Curves Fitness Centers became the largest fitness and health club franchise in the world by challenging the *value profile* of the full-service health club. Traditional health clubs catered to men and women, and offered a full range of equipment at a high monthly fee. Curves was positioned as a women's gym, providing a total body workout in 30 minutes at one-third of the monthly fee. Its equipment was especially designed for women and arranged in a circle to encourage conversation; timed music moved participants from machine to machine in a way that made the overall experience more enjoyable.

The main growth pathway followed by Curves was the delivery of a different profile of attributes from that of traditional full-service health clubs. However, they also overcame barriers to consumption among women and, to a lesser degree, satisfied latent or unmet needs for a disciplined workout with social reinforcement. Their offering was an innovative arrangement of standard elements found in many health clubs. However, Curves offers a deeper lesson: the more growth pathways involved with an innovation initiative, the more compelling and integrated the value proposition, and the harder it is for rivals to copy or leapfrog.

This chapter posed a strategic choice that is usually implicit: either take a *reactive* approach and wait for opportunities to arrive, or probe each of the 12 pathways to identify the best opportunities and then pursue them ahead of others. Growth leaders take a disciplined approach to the 12 pathways that balances *divergence* – to widen the search for the best opportunities – with *convergence* on those that best serve the growth strategy. The value of discipline was first highlighted by Peter Drucker (1985), who viewed innovation as a skill that could be learned and practiced, similar to playing a musical instrument. He believed that innovation was about devising a systematic way of identifying opportunities that provide new value for customers and exploiting them with disciplined work: "What all successful entrepreneurs I have met have in common is not a certain kind of personality, but a commitment to the systematic practice of innovation" (Drucker 1985, p. 110).

Successfully exercising innovation discipline requires an investment of significant resources and leadership commitment. The process for exercising opportunity-seeking discipline that we observe among growth leaders is shown in Figure 6.2.

*Step one: diagnose the current portfolio of growth opportunities.* To assemble and display this portfolio, start by casting a wide net well beyond the

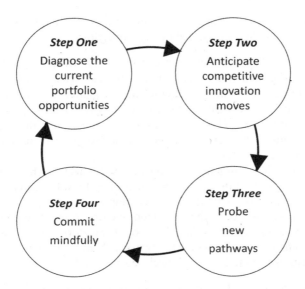

**Figure 6.2**     Which way should you grow?

R&D projects in the development portfolio. For example, what business model opportunities are being worked on by the supply chain team, the sales team, and the pricing group?

When the projects are compiled (with an estimate of the potential resources required and future gains), assign them to a pathway or combination of pathways. Helpful diagnostic questions are:

- Which pathways are getting the largest share of total resources? Why is the dominant pathway attracting the most resources? Should it?
- What share of the opportunities are small-*i*, adjacencies or BIG-*I* innovations? What does this say about the risk appetite of the business?
- What share of the growth opportunities are aligned with (and reinforcing of) the customer value proposition?

A revealing transition question, that helps set up the next step, is whether the business is following or breaking away from the industry conventional wisdom (Govindarajan and Trimble 2005)?

*Step two: anticipate competitors moves.* This takes a targeted version of competitive intelligence, guided by these questions:

- Which pathways are our direct rivals emphasizing? What can we learn from their financial and patent filings? What skill sets are they recruiting and hiring? What clues can we gather from the pattern of their merger and acquisitions (M&A) activity? What experiments are they conducting? This information is often collected during routine competitive intelligence, but needs to be interpreted with an innovation opportunity lens.
- If we are not the organic growth leader in the sector, who is, and what are they doing differently? This firm must be watched carefully for ideas on possible better practices to adopt.
- A tougher question is the likelihood of entry from outside the industry. What emerging technologies could transform our industry, and which firms or countries are likely to use them to gain entry? Adjacent industries need to be especially closely watched.

The primary aim of this step is to anticipate and prepare for the moves and countermoves of the direct rivals. This will indicate which growth projects should be accelerated to avoid missing an opportunity and becoming an imitator.

*Step three: probe new pathways.* A basic premise of the growth pathways approach to strategic innovation is that most firms in an industry will pursue growth along the same pathways (especially pathway 7: develop innovative new products, services, or platforms). Momentum, past experience and the need to match the moves of rivals sustain this reality. Our counterargument is that shifting some resources to innovation pathways no one else in the industry is pursuing, may at a minimum yield profitable incremental growth, but could also be a game-changer. A further argument for probing a wider set of pathways is the logical extension of the strategic thinking exercise that poses the question: "How would someone from outside the industry attack us?" This will probably not be a direct attack.

To carry out this step is to pick a pathway that is not being pursued, and then conjecture how it might be pursued or combined with moves along other pathways. This is the logic underlying a further premise of the pathways model, that innovations simultaneously pursuing combinations of pathways yield larger opportunities that are harder to copy.

Reinforcing this premise is the notion that innovations are also part of systems that are greater than the sum of their parts (Kumar 2013, p. 52): "offerings based on integrated innovation of multiple parts of a system are likely to have greater value." A powerful example is the sequence of systems innovations by Apple with the iPod and iTunes, the iPhone and the App Store, and later the iPad. These innovations collectively reinvented the music business, the mobile devices sector, and the tablet computers industry.

*Step four: commit mindfully.* During this step, exploration and the exercise of curiosity shifts to committing resources to attractive opportunities, but in a careful, deliberate manner that respects the inevitable risks. The level of risk depends on where the opportunity lies on the small *i*–BIG *I* spectrum. The further toward the BIG *I* and transformative innovation end of this spectrum, the greater the need for mindful approaches to development. Risks can be contained, but not eliminated, with methods such as a trial-and-error experimentation to learn, investments in real options, for example, small R&D projects or taking small, toehold stakes in startup firms, or teaming up with a complementary firm in a joint venture. The ultimate aim is to prepare the organization to act when the time is ripe for the innovation.

When the growth-seeking process is done well, the organization will have honed its dynamic sensing and seizing capabilities, and will be better able to innovate with alacrity and confidence, and grow faster than rivals.

## NOTE

1.   There is an emerging consensus that a business model enables the coherent implementation of a strategy (Wirtz et al. 2016). Beyond this point, there is little agreement. Some authors (Osterwalder and Pigneur 2010) go so far as to embed the entirety of the customer value proposition and customer segments within the business model. This is an overly expansive approach that blurs the important distinction between the outside-in framing of the customer value proposition and the inside-out aspect of a business model. See also, Girotra and Netessine (2014).

# 7 Strategy formulation starts from the outside in

The limitations of traditional approaches to strategy formulation were sharply exposed during the global pandemic, as companies had to quickly adjust their strategies in the face of extreme uncertainty. Some companies were more successful in making this pivot, in part because they began their strategy making from the outside in. They assessed their fast-changing situation by first taking the viewpoint of their external stakeholders, rivals, and key influencers to understand their strategic options and constraints. Consequently, they were better prepared for greater turbulence. The purpose of this chapter is to diagnose this approach to strategy formulation and explain how it yields superior long-run performance.

Many organizations, including publicly traded companies, follow a prescribed strategy planning process. The leadership team collectively decides the strategies, resource commitments, budget, and operating plans once a year, and then manages operations in accordance with these choices. This process is often launched with a strengths/weaknesses/opportunities/threats (SWOT) analysis (Mintzberg 1990; Hill and Westbrook 1997). The strengths and weaknesses analyses are prone to using a self-referential internal mind-set where it is tempting to classify as a strength something the firm does especially well, but perhaps not better than a competitor. The opportunities and threats components bring in the outside environment, but are often framed narrowly within the context of the current strategy.

In the traditional strategy model the questions are, "How can we sell more? Improve our asset productivity? How else can we deploy our capabilities?" These are important and relevant questions, but prematurely narrow and constrain the strategy dialogue. Instead, it is better to start by stepping outside the boundaries, resources, and limitations of the organization as it is, and ask, "How are the needs of our present and prospective customers changing? What new competitors can meet these needs? What emerging technologies could disrupt our industry?" These questions introduce an outside-in perspective, and by switching the frame or vantage point they strengthen the strategy formulation process (Brandenberger 2017).

This chapter begins by contrasting the outside-in and inside-out approaches to strategy formulation to show the advantages of an iterative strategy process that starts with a wide-angle, outside-in perspective. Then we show that this process is consistent with three cognate concepts: dynamic capabilities, design thinking, and market orientation. Finally, we describe four supportive properties of organizations that are necessary to fully realize the value of an outside-in approach.

## Which path to strategy?

An illustration of the differences between the outside-in versus inside-out approaches comes when an innovation process starts with a product or technology map emphasizing product features, versus starting the same process with a customer experience map that focuses on the benefits the features should provide (Kim et al. 2018). A big drawback of starting with a technology map is limiting the options to what is possible, versus launching a broader quest for what will be needed. This perhaps explains the difficulties of healthcare technology start-ups that received more than $8 billion in funding in 2018, while only a few of their products have succeeded and been integrated deeply into the labyrinthine medical system. A contributor to this string of failures is the mind-set that the development process is primarily a technical puzzle. Successes such as Omada Health (Unger 2018), which provides online counseling for people with chronic diseases, resonate because they were designed by people who were trained to think of patients first and emphasized improving their total experience.

The outside-in approach is an orientation to strategic issues and a *decision-making priority*, given direction and meaning as a *mental model* that is empathetic to external stakeholders and agents. The internal representations/mental models of both the leadership team and the key implementers determine the way strategic choices and investments are made (Adner and Helfat 2003; Narayan et al. 2011).

This approach to strategy-formulation is compatible with those aspects of the dynamic capabilities framework emphasizing the need to, "define managerial traits, management systems and organizational designs that will keep the organization alert to opportunities and threats, enable it to execute on new opportunities, and then to constantly morph to stay on top" (Teece 2009, p. 206). A dynamic capability is not an ad hoc resolution of a single problem, but a repeatable and deeply embedded set of skills and knowledge exercised through organization processes. These capabilities enable organizations to *sense* opportunities sooner than their rivals do, *seize* them more effectively, and support the organizational *transformation* needed to stay ahead. When guided by a clear strategic vision, they enable the organization to adapt to turbulent and uncertain market conditions (Teece 2007).

An early delineation of the outside-in and inside-out approaches to strategy making was that of Emery and Trist (1965). Their causal textures theory denoted the two-way links between an organization and its environment as "transactional relations that were either inside out (planning) or outside in (learning)" (Emery and Trist 1965, p. 25). They posited that organizations influenced their situation in relation to the environment, and were influenced by this environment. This was the genesis of the social ecology approach to understanding external environments (Ramirez and Selsky 2016), with an emphasis on turbulence-induced uncertainty, which is better dealt with by starting from the outside in.

Within the field of strategy, the early emphasis of influential concepts and approaches favored inside-out thinking, with the popularity in practice of SWOT and the early emphasis on the resource-based view (RBV) of the firm. The basis of the RBV is that scarce, inimitable, and valuable resources (such as patents, facilities, and brands) exist to be used (Barney 1991). It follows that the task of management is to improve and fully exploit these resources (Makadok 2001). This leads to an emphasis on internal efficiency improvements and short-term cost-cutting moves. This perspective can prematurely anchor the strategy dialogue to what exists now, versus what might be possible in the future.

The balance of emphasis began shifting toward outside-in approaches with the advent of dynamic capabilities frameworks (as noted previously) and a further formalization of the approach by Wind (2008) and Day and Moorman (2010) that built upon the cumulating evidence of the performance benefits of a market or customer orientation of an organization. There was also a reinforcing desire to provide a counterweight to such decision biases as overconfidence, excessive optimism and confirmation bias, informed by only the facts that supported prevailing beliefs. Decision theorists (Lovallo and Kahneman 2003; Kahneman 2011) found that an inside perspective inherently neglects competitive reactions to initiatives a company has never attempted before, such as forecasting new product sales or estimating the profit rewards of cost cutting.

## Cognate concepts

An outside-in perspective is compatible with design thinking and market (or customer) orientation, and gains from the advances in research into their antecedents and consequences. Design thinking (Knight et al. 2020) takes a *bottom-up* emphasis on individual contributors and projects, whereas market-orientation research takes a top-down perspective. Although each concept is converging on the same domain of strategic issues, they are far from a rapprochement judging from the lack of cross-referencing in their respective scholarship. When taken together, these two concepts usefully illuminate and inform the outside-in approach to strategy.

*Market orientation.* This concept has been a defining element of the marketing discipline for more than 60 years. Market orientation lacked both theoretical rigor and empirical validation until 1990 when two teams of scholars independently established the boundaries, antecedents, and performance consequences of the construct. Kohli and Jaworski (1990, p. 3, original emphases), defined market orientation as, "the organization-wide *generation* of market intelligence pertaining to current and future customer needs, *dissemination* of the intelligence across departments, and organization-side *responsiveness* to it." This behavioral definition has a decided capabilities emphasis, but does not address how the insights extracted from the intelligence are to be used. Concurrently, Narver and Slater (1990, p. 22) defined market orientation as, "the organizational culture that most effectively and efficiently creates the necessary behavior for the creation of superior value for buyers and thus, continuous superior performance for the business." They then created a persistent confusion by proposing that a market orientation, "consists of three behavioral components – customer orientation, competitor orientation, and inter-functional coordination." The problem is that these three components are also embedded in the values, beliefs, and mind-sets that shape the culture.

A resolution of the culture or behavior question was suggested by Homburg and Pflesser (2000). Since the construct of market orientation is generally operationalized by the behaviors that are manifested, they propose that these behaviors reflect an underlying organization culture. This is consistent with the literature on culture change in organizations, which holds that behaviors reflect the prevailing culture and that the culture slowly changes to accord with, and make sense of, the behaviors (Kotter 2012). However, at any particular time the culture and the behaviors in the Kohli and Jaworski (1990) definition may not be congruent. In an era where the rate of change is accelerating this is increasingly likely.

The center of gravity of the marketing concept has shifted toward an emphasis on customers, rather than all the players in the market ecosystem, including competitors and channel partners. This reflects the natural gravitational pull of marketers toward the constituency they know best and acknowledges their assigned role within the organization as the voice of the customer. There is some recognition of the constraining role of competitors in customer choice processes. Customer-orientated concepts and tools, such as consideration sets, product concept tests, conjoint analysis, and lead user analyses, incorporate the competitive set when choice judgments are made. This does not account for the strategies and intentions of current or potential competitors, any potential threats from emerging businesses models, or consequences of the lowering of barriers to entry owing to digital advances.

Notwithstanding the mounting evidence of the performance gains from adopting or achieving a market orientation (Kirca et al. 2005; Morgan et al. 2009; Palmatier et al. 2019) this outside-in orientation has not always been endorsed as a guide to strategic choices and actions. Widely publicized dissenting views about the primacy of customers came from Steve Jobs (Isaacson 2011) and Howard Schultz, the CEO of Starbucks, "Don't just give the customers what they ask for" (Schultz and Yang 1997, p. 12). Robert Lutz, then the Vice-Chairman of Chrysler, was especially dismissive of reliance on consumer inputs into the auto design process, "Let's face it, the customer in this business … is usually, at best, just a rear-view mirror. He can tell you what he likes about the choices that are already out there" (Flint 1997, p. 84). These thought leaders did not deny the need to listen to customers; they simply found it deficient as a guide to action. These visionaries were acute observers of market shifts, with an innate understanding of the meaning and value of a superior customer experience. Some argue that these firms teach rather than learn, "by (building) consensus for innovative concepts of value rather than analyzing and reacting to buyers" (Humphreys and Carpenter 2018, p. 145; 2019). More likely, visionaries both learn and teach.

A limitation of marketing and strategy research has been the focus on successful survivors. Archival studies tracking all entries and exits into a market find the failure rate among "visionaries" to be high (Golder and Tellis 2002). The successes were blessed with leaders who were highly observant of customer reactions while learning from the failures of their predecessors. Thus, Howard Schulz envisioned his original concept of a third place by observing customer communities in Italian coffee houses (Schultz and Yang 1997). Similarly, Steve Jobs saw more deeply the possibilities of the personal computer.

*Design thinking.* At the heart of this approach is the motivation to improve an organization's offering and interactions with key stakeholders, through an iterative process of creative problem solving. While there are many variants of the design-thinking process (Brown 2008; Martin 2009), all embody the same principles and adopt the same general process. There are typically four iterative steps in the human-centered process of generating new ideas and insights through empathetic listening and then narrowing the focus through testing (O'Reilly and Binns 2019):

1. Empathize by deeply understanding customer's problems, often through observation. The focus is on achieving connection and even intimacy with users (Bason and Austin 2019).
2. Define the real problem the customer has while being open to changing this definition as new insights emerge.
3. Ideate using brainstorming and other tools to generate alternative solutions. The aim is to get beyond satisficing answers to find truly innovative ideas.
4. Prototype and test with users, listen carefully to their reactions, and use their reactions to redefine the problem.

The dominant feature of design thinking is user-centeredness and involvement. Empathy is considered the primary means of achieving this user-centeredness (Micheli et al. 2019), where empathy is referred to as "the core value of human-centeredness" (Carlgren et al. 2016, p. 42). For design thinkers, empathy means taking the perspective of another and understanding what they regard as meaningful. Beyond being a people-first approach, design thinking is also an antidote to the inherent constrictions of linear problem-solving, by using trial-and-error learning and encouraging a tolerance for ambiguity and failure. This approach is best followed by a diverse team representing different skills, interests and capabilities.

Design thinking is sometimes termed "outside the box" thinking, as designers seek to overcome the constraints of dominant designs and approaches. One feature is the falsification of previous assumptions based on inside-out thinking, setting the stage for ideas that reflect the genuine constraints and facets of the problem. The design process is firmly based on generating a holistic and empathetic understanding of the real problems people face, and inherently involves ambiguous and subjective considerations. This contrasts with a solely scientific approach to testing user's needs and emotions.

Design thinking has evolved independently from marketing, while sharing many aspects with market orientation. First, is an obvious commonality of methods: market research and design research share many qualitative methods (Beckman 2020), but design thinkers could certainly benefit from advances in customer experience mapping, latent needs analysis methods, and focus groups. Second, the effective implementation of both approaches/mind-sets requires strong leadership (Bason and Austin 2019) to help their organizations think differently: practice empathy, change mind-sets, and navigate ambiguity. Leaders must be advocates of the respective approaches and encourage adoption through example. Finally, although design thinking appears coherent and cohesive, it shares with the concept of market orientation the problem of diverse perspectives and critics. Some view design thinking as an organizational attribute, while others conceive it at the individual or team level; some focus on design as culture, while others highlight the tools and the process. A recent review (Micheli 2019) characterized the construct as suffering from polysemy (the existence of many possible meanings).

*Other cognate approaches.* The soil for outside-in perspectives on strategic issues is fertile, judging by the level of activity. Two approaches – "jobs-to-be-done" and "working backwards" – have arisen independently with little acknowledgment of either market orientation or design thinking. Yet both share many features and tackle similar issues.

The basis of the "jobs-to-be-done" approach is that: "*our long-held maxim – that the crux of innovation is knowing more and more about the customer is wrong ... Understanding customers does not drive innovation success... understanding customer jobs does.*" (Christensen et al. 2016a, 2016b, p. 10, original emphasis). According to these advocates a well-defined job is, "*very different from the traditional marketing concept of 'needs' because it entails a much higher degree of specificity about what you're solving for... needs are important to consumers, but they generally provide only the vaguest of direction to innovators as to how to solve them*" (Christensen et al. 2016a, 2016b, p. 22, original emphasis).

Jeff Bezos, the founder and Chairman of Amazon.com advocates what he calls a "working backward" mentality (CB Insights 2020, p. 2, original emphasis): "*Rather than ask what we are good at and what else can we do with that skill, you ask, who are our customers? What do they need? And then you say we're going to give that to them regardless of whether we have the skills to do so, and we will learn these skills no matter how long it takes.*" Bezos attributes this approach to the success of Amazon in meeting the needs of customers for Web services by offering access to its cloud computing network and for a more convenient reading experience with the Kindle. This is a central element of their stated mission to be "Earth's Most Customer Centric Company (or EMC3)."

The apparent origin of this approach was Steve Jobs, who once said that, "you have to start with the customer experience and work backwards towards the technology." It is put to work within Amazon when they are developing or updating new products, by first requiring the writing of an internal, two-page or less press release describing the end product, based on solving a specific customer problem. The press release has to be written without technical jargon and is focused on the benefits to the target customers. The results are greater empathy and deeper understanding of customer needs, and a more effective communication of the offering. It is worth noting, in contrast to other approaches, that there is little emphasis on customer life-time value and more emphasis on creating an emotional connection across the portfolio of offerings. It has been credited with Amazon becoming the third ranked, "most innovative" company based on the innovation premium investors grant them (Dyer and Gregersen 2017).


## An iterative approach to strategy formulation

Strategy making seeks the best balance of exploratory and exploitative activities (March 1991; Benner and Tushman 2003) to generate superior current earnings while funding continued growth. This is not an either/ or dichotomy as implied by the advice to choose either a *supply-push* approach to innovation – developing technology and then finding or creating a market – versus a demand-pull approach by surfacing the latent problems of customers and then solving them (Pisano 2015). This false choice is premised on the assumptions that customers lack imagination and that a demand-pull approach raises the "risk of missing out on technologies for which markets have not yet emerged" (Pisano 2015, p. 49). Instead, both approaches need to be effectively combined and sequenced for maximum effectiveness.

The process starts with outside-in questions to frame a broad context for inside-out considerations of resources to be leveraged, capabilities to be exercised, and constraints to be overcome. Outside-in thinking respects but subordinates these inside-out factors within a wider setting. Each iterative cycle begins with a wide-angle, outside-in lens, creating new insights and deeper questions to feed the next cycle through cumulative learning. This strategy process is shown in Figure 7.1, with illustrative questions from the outside-in versus inside-out perspectives.

A wide outside-in lens (Adner 2017) encourages looking further into the future and considering all the players in the surrounding ecosystem, and their next moves and countermoves. It overcomes the myopic emphasis of inside-out companies on the short-run moves of their direct rivals, while overlooking their long-run positioning moves or the threat of potential entrants from adjacent sectors. By starting with a wide-angle lens the leadership team has a more deeply informed view of the past actions, intentions, and likely reactions of the most influential elements of the ecosystem, and how they will interact with one another. This requires

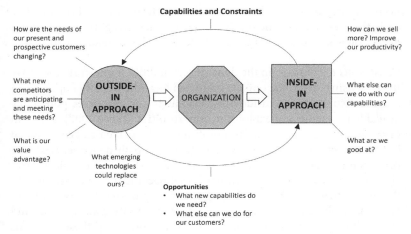

**Figure 7.1**    An iterative approach to strategy formulation

an objectivity (and skepticism) about the future that challenges comfortable assumptions and illusions.

The benefits of an expansive outside-in approach were illustrated by Tuli et al. (2007) in their study of how B2B firms define a customer solution. They found the prevailing inside-out view was that, "solutions are bundles of products and services that help us sell more" (Tuli et al. 2007, p. 6). By contrast, the emerging outside-in view was that, "the purpose of a solution is to help our customers succeed to our mutual benefit, by enhancing performance, decreasing their risks, and reducing their total life cycle costs" (Tuli et al. 2007, p. 6). A subsequent test of their model of customer solutions (Worm et al. 2017), described solutions as: (1) built on deeply understanding customer requirements, (2) taking the form of an output-based performance contract that delivers on customer-specified metrics, (3) customized to customer activities and/or processes, and (4) providing post-deployment support.

Superior strategic moves emerge when the outside-in approach is closely integrated with inside-out considerations, so they reinforce each other. The dualism of yin and yang in ancient Chinese philosophy is an apt expression of the desired interaction. This dualism describes how seemingly contrary forces or approaches are complementary; one giving rise to the other. In order to achieve organizational balance, both approaches need to be deployed, but always starting from the outside in. Each iterative cycle that begins from the outside in creates new insights and generates deeper questions that feed the next cycle through cumulative learning.

*Constraints to consider.* In the dynamic capabilities framework, the move from "sensing" from the outside in, to "seizing" the potential opportunities must consider the inside-out capabilities and resources potentially available to pursue and exploit the opportunities (Teece 2007). What an organization can realistically accomplish is both enabled and constrained by the trajectory of the organization (creating path dependencies) and prior commitments to strategies and resources. Future strategic choices also involve investment commitments that become future constraints to the extent they are irreversible. Jeff Bezos emphasized this in his letter to Amazon shareholders in 2016: "Such decisions are consequential and irreversible or nearly irreversible – one-way doors – and these decisions must be made methodically, carefully, slowly, with great deliberation and consultation. If you walk through and don't like what you see on the other side, you can't go back to where you were before."

Commitments to past strategic choices also impose constraints on existing routines, structures, culture norms, beliefs and behaviors, and human resources. Seizing future opportunities requires deeper commitment that put constraints on future actions, so it may be expedient to maintain flexibility with methods such as partnering, outsourcing, and building multipurpose facilities and capabilities.

*Strategy as an input and outcome of the process.* The mutual dependency of the strategy formulation process and the content of the strategy is revealed in the Rumelt (2011) specification of a "good" strategy. What he terms the "kernel" of this strategy has a "diagnosis, a guiding policy, and a coherent action" (Rumelt 2011, p. 7). The guiding policy specifies how the obstacles and opportunities identified in the diagnosis are to be dealt with. "It is like a signpost, marking the direction forward, but no defining the details of the trip" (Rumelt 2011, p. 7). Thus the guiding policy is either constricted, or expanded and enriched by the breadth of the diagnosis. Coherent actions are the integrated policies, resource commitments, and functional actions needed to implement the guiding policy. By contrast, bad strategies fail to recognize or interpret the challenges to the organization and confuse goals with the specific actions to be taken.

# 8    Enabling outside-in strategy making

Many properties potentially distinguish the organizations best equipped to successfully formulate and implement outside-in strategies. Some were originally investigated as the antecedents of market orientation. However, there was scant recognition in the original formulation of market orientation (Jaworski and Kohli 1993) of the possibilities and limitations inherent in the portfolio of ordinary and dynamic capabilities. The antecedents that were studied at that time were: (1) top management emphasis, (2) interdepartmental dynamics of conflict and connectedness, and (3) the degree of formalization and centralization of organizational systems and rewards. This reflected the state of organizational research of the era, which was static and structural. This conceptualization spawned a number of empirical studies. A meta-analysis of 114 of these studies (Kirca et al. 2005) concluded that leadership emphasis and internal processes had more influence than organizational structure variables.

Advances in the cognate fields and organization theory have since found three further properties of organizations that are conducive to the successful formulation of strategies from the outside in: (1) *an empathetic orientation*, (2) catalyzed by collective *curiosity*, and (3) an emphasis on gaining *foresight* and looking forward. These three properties are dependent on the role modeling and emphasis placed by the *leadership team* on outside-in approaches. These hypothesized relations are illustrated in Figure 8.1.

We diagnose these properties to identify the indicators and relationships to be assessed at the organizational level. For example, there is suggestive evidence that, because curiosity and empathy are closely interwoven at the personal level, they might be related at the organizational level. The argument is that empathy occurs when a person is deeply curious about, and invested in, the experience of someone else.

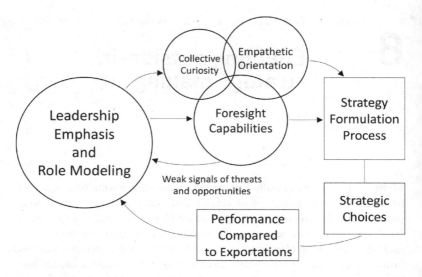

**Figure 8.1**     Properties of outside-in organizations

## Leadership emphasis and role modeling

An outside-in mind-set and orientation to strategic issues should not be the sole purview of the chief executive officer (CEO). In order to be effective at guiding the organization, this mind-set needs to pervade the senior leadership team, to express the tone at the top, and consistently convey this decision priority. The qualities that distinguish vigilant leadership teams (Day and Schoemaker 2008) are very applicable. These teams focus externally and are open to diverse views; they apply strategic foresight and probe for second-order effects, and encourage others to explore widely by creating a culture of discovery. These leadership teams create the psychological space and give permission to all levels of the organization, to share perspectives about relevant issues beyond their immediate domain. Employees at the periphery of the organization are often closer to the early signals of looming threats or latent opportunities, and must feel comfortable that they will have an open hearing when raising concerns or suggesting strategy initiatives.

The most influential members of vigilant leadership teams are strong communicators who collaborate with other functions and serve as credible advisors to the CEO on strategic issues (Leinwand and Mainardi 2013). Within this leadership team there are many competing demands on their scarce collective attention (Ocasio 1997), so there needs to be a credible advocate for an outside-in approach. This could be the chief marketing officer (CMO) (Boyd et al. 2010) or the chief strategy officer. The position and influence of this advocate will vary between firms, depending on how siloed the organization is with their strategic activities.

Role modeling entails leading by example, adopting behaviors and actions that endorse, affirm and validate an outside-in orientation, and being regular and consistent. Unless the entire organization sees a continued commitment and receives a consistent signal from the leadership team about this orientation, it will probably revert to making strategic decisions from the inside out. Many centripetal forces converge to encourage employees to look outward from their firm-based positions: (1) positive reinforcement, from seeing the immediate, positive results gained by increasing the efficiency of existing resources; (2) competing priorities – within the organization internal concerns about resource allocation, budgeting, and functional turf wars can easily become the most pressing priorities; and (3) self-preservation. This primordial instinct naturally reinforces an inside-out orientation since the outside-in approach may require the firm to reinvent itself, and this change will probably be disruptive and threatening.

An example of the ability of a forceful leader to shape the orientation is the transformation of Ryanair. This European ultra-low-cost airline has been among the most profitable airlines in the world by offering the best price, achieved by a relentless focus on fixed asset utilization (the amount of time airplanes are in the air). High utilization was achieved with an operating model that did not permit allocated seating while imposing rigid boarding procedures and harsh baggage limits (Meehan 2017). Their rigid cost containment model was seen by customers as harsh and unfriendly, but was defended by the combative CEO Michael O'Leary who argued, "People say the customer is always right, but you know what – they're not. Sometimes they are wrong and they need to be told so" (Meehan 2017, p. 3). A challenge to this approach began during the 2013 shareholder meeting when some investors questioned whether the macho culture and strict service policies were deterring customers. These blunt critiques and the reality that rival easyJet was gaining ground with more customer-friendly policies, prompted the hiring of their first CMO. The new CMO was also charged with developing the airline's digital capabilities which had fallen behind minimum acceptable levels. The CMO was persuaded to join the airline by Michael O'Leary's sincerity and commitment to addressing the problems and the willingness of the leadership team to experiment and change.

A rapid series of changes – notably the move to allocated seating – culminated in their December 2014 statement of "Always Getting Better" that aspired to, "fix the things customers did not like ... [while] improving the customer and digital experiences." Three years after launching this initiative and building a superior digital capability, Ryanair revenues had increased by 37 percent, and profits more than doubled. During this period the load factor rose from 87 percent to 95 percent, while Ryanair continued to offer the lowest fares. O'Leary summed up the success of this outside-in transformation by saying, "If I'd know it would work so well, I'd have done it years ago" (Meehan 2017, p. 6).

### An empathetic orientation

This orientation is manifested when a competitor analysis begins by trying to see the company through the eyes of the competitor's leadership team. The starting point is a deep immersion in available intelligence followed by role playing of each of the leaders of the competitor to anticipate their likely response to possible strategic moves (Zenko 2015). This is a variant of the "red team" exercise used by the military, and sensitizes the organization to threat indicators before they reach top management's radar.

Empathy is implied in becoming market oriented, often with the exhortation to stand in the customers shoes or "staple yourself to an order," but this connection needs to make explicit as suggested by the following quote (Young 2015, p. 3):

> Empathy is an understanding you develop about another person. Empathizing is the use of that understanding – an action ... Empathy gives you the ability to try on that person's perspective ... But empathy is hard to achieve, ... People try to act empathetic – to take some's perspective, to walk in his shoes – without first taking the time to develop empathy.

Empathy is an elastic term and becomes imprecise when stretched to apply to organizations. It could mean a supportive workplace culture, built on skills of empathic listening to colleagues that collectively inspires openness and trust. This requires (Kets de Vries 2016) an enhanced ability to imagine the emotional reactions and experience of others. An *instrumental* application of empathy is the training of customer-contact representatives to appreciate customer's feelings and understand their frustrations, to improve the customer experience. This is advocated as a way of making the customer feel valued.

A more relevant use of empathy is a shared sense of what is going on in the environment, guided by connecting with people outside the organizational boundaries and adopting their perspective (Patnaik 2009). This *diagnostic* application of empathy requires an external orientation throughout the organization. When embedded in an organization it becomes a strategic priority and a cultural value.

## Catalyzed by curiosity

Collective curiosity encourages the asking of questions to be explored, and directs attention outside the company (Gino 2018). It is a key ingredient for understanding the past (what were the real reasons for our success?), a stimulus for a deeper understanding of present realities (what are the reasons for the marketplace anomalies we are seeing – are they an indicator of changes in customer needs and requirements?), and a more informed anticipation of the future. Isaac Asimov, the prolific science writer, caught the essence of curiosity with his observation, "The most exciting phrase to hear in science, the one that heralds new discoveries, is not 'Eureka (I found it)' but 'That's funny'" (Applewhite and Frothingham 2003, p. 469).

Sustained curiosity throughout an organization creates strategic options to be exercised when the time is right. This helped Sephora, the global beauty retailer, keep its momentum during the pandemic. In the lockdown period their unique blend of in-store ambience, personalized experience and sample-as-you-go was no protection from challenges by rival Ulta or Amazon. Fortunately, Sephora's management had long been intrigued by the adoption of gamification in the adjoining life-style categories of exercise clubs and dating sites. Adding the game mechanisms of point-scoring, friendly competition with others, and rewards, increased engagement, which they had confirmed with several tests. They had also experimented with ways to further engage clients through online and mobile platforms; their Virtual Artist helped clients "try on" make-up products through their mobile phones.

Sephora's disciplined exercise of curiosity gave them an edge over rivals in pivoting their strategy to respond to an online retail world. They accelerated their investments in Augmented Reality and facial recognition to fast track a project to gamify beauty. Sephora clients could try make-up with friends in different locations, experiment with new products, walk through a virtual store, and talk with a live beauty consultant.

Collective curiosity is shaped by the actions of the leadership team. They can encourage curiosity by being inquisitive themselves and approaching the future with an openness to new possibilities. Conversely, leaders can discourage curiosity in the mistaken belief they will avoid making the organization harder to manage, and seeking efficiency to the detriment of curiosity-driven experimentation.

Abductive reasoning (Dong et al. 2016) can enhance collective curiosity. The aim of abduction is to generate new knowledge by generating competing hypotheses, and by abandoning old convictions and seeking better ones. As Martin (2009b, p. 25) observed, "When you are facing something that doesn't obey the previous rules or have some data (but not enough to be inductive), you make an inference to the best explanation of what is going on." This logical leap of the mind leads to new ideas, and these ideas can only be proven to be correct or valid by the unfolding of time and future events. That is, abductive reasoning encourages organizations to pursue ideas beyond the tried and true. There are two types of abduction: explanatory and innovative. In either type, there is an observation which could be an anomalous or surprising event, or a desired, intended outcome. With explanatory abduction, a new rule is inferred to explain the surprise. With innovative abduction, a new strategic move is imagined that will possibly achieve the result. Also in either type, curiosity is aroused to find the new rule or strategy move. The aim is to generate with the most plausible and parsimonious explanation for the observation. This explanation becomes a hypothesis to be tested with deductive reasoning.

## Forward looking

An outside-in approach is more about preparedness (to capture opportunities faster than others while parrying threats) than prescience. The aim is to anticipate and understand events and trends, to avoid losing later degrees of freedom of strategic action and then being forced to act defensively. Foresight tools and approaches help organizations to understand, absorb, and adapt to the inherent uncertainty of environmental trends and forces. We can distinguish between state uncertainty (how will the environment change, how will attitudes toward privacy of customer data change, and will autonomous vehicles dominate the market?), and response uncertainty about the likely impact of strategic moves such as launching a new business model or change to a subscription pricing model (Vecchiato 2015). Whereas state uncertainty demands foresight through the detection and interpretation of weak signals, response uncertainty may be resolved by hindsight approaches that seek patterns in big data or a series of market experiments. However, the utility of hindsight approaches depends on whether the environmental forces operating in the past are likely to persist into the future. Given the mounting turbulence in markets accentuated by digital technologies, the emphasis of strategic thinking should shift toward foresight.

To achieve a forward-looking posture, organizations invest in foresight. These investments are first made in the organizational arrangements (for example, creating a separate foresight unit, forming global scouting teams, or installing precursor units in geographic outposts). A return on these investments is realized through further investments in the disciplined search for opportunities, anticipatory competitor analysis, scenario development, and monitoring or creating a portfolio of experiments and early-stage investments.

The nature of these foresight investments depends on the firm and the industry requirements. Unilever, the global consumer goods giant, prioritizes investments in insights and analytics capabilities (ranging from monitoring social media to mining data from their consumer hot lines), and then interpreting and widely disseminating the insights (Van Den Driest et al. 2016). They have an advanced AI platform for querying their databases with natural language questions from all parts of the organization. The insights group reports directly to the leadership team as a signal of their commitment to outside-in thinking.

This forward-looking property of organizations embeds an outside-in approach within the more general, dynamic sensing capability (Teece 2009). This capability enables an organization to spot, interpret, and pursue potential opportunities. This entails the exercise of constant vigilance through scanning, searching, and exploring, including probing latent customer needs, monitoring competitive threats from adjacent sectors, and collecting timely intelligence about every aspect of the market ecosystem. Successful sensing is achieving through two interrelated learning processes that serve as dynamic sub-capabilities (Day and Schoemaker 2016). The peripheral vision sub-capability is activated to capture sooner than rivals the early signals of potential opportunities and nascent threats. This sub-capability determines how widely to scope (and what issues to address first), and how actively to scan. All managers scan, but often do so passively. They are continually exposed to a wealth of data, from the fuzzy impressions of trade rumors to firmer evidence from their dashboard of performance metrics. By contrast, active scanning is often abductive, reflecting intense curiosity that pushes the scan out to the periphery of the organization.

The vigilant learning dynamic sub-capability enables interpreting and understanding the weak signals of threats and opportunities, and requires a willingness to act on partial information. Vigilance means a heightened state of awareness and alertness that helps decision making and the allocation of attention to the future. Thus, learning about new market opportunities requires a willingness to be immersed in the lives of past, present, and prospective customers to learn how they process data, an open-minded approach to exploring latent needs and learning from lead users, and extracting early insights from data analytics.

The close parallelism of outside-in approaches, market orientation, and dynamic capabilities thinking is suggested by the following quote: "The three basic routines of the sensing capability are: (i) generating market intelligence, (ii) disseminating market intelligence (Kogut [and] Zander, 1992), and (iii) responding to market intelligence (Teece, 2007). These routines are related to kindred routines in the dynamic capabilities literature" (Pavlou and Sawny 2011, p. 250). This quote takes us full circle to our earlier conclusion about the convergence of cognate concepts toward the same outside-in approach to strategy making.

## Performance gains from outside-in approaches

There is no single conclusive study of the benefits of adopting an outside-in approach to strategy formulation. Fortunately, there has been an accumulation of positive results that are steadily filling in the missing pieces of the jigsaw puzzle picture of a multifaceted relationship. These supportive results can be grouped by the predominant performance parameter being studied: organizational resilience and agility, vigilance and foresight, and market and financial performance.

### Organizational resilience and agility

The concept of resilient organizations was initially based on studies of companies that had successfully emerged from sharp economic down-turns (Gulati 2009). Those companies with an inside-out mind-set were found to be less resilient in turbulent times, "than those organized around an outside-in mindset that starts with the marketplace, then looks to cre-atively deliver on market opportunities. Outside in maximizes customer value – and produces more supple organizations" (Gulati 2009, p. 231). The emphasis of this study was on designing organizations to become more resilient by breaking down barriers that impede action, building bridges across divisions, and crating networks of collaborations.

The architecture of inside-out organizations dictated a strategic focus on the attributes of offerings, and an orientation toward selling products or services rather than towards customers and the problems they are trying to solve. Gulati proposed five levers for organizational transformation: *coordination* (to connect and restructure silos to enable swift responses), *cooperation* (among employees), *clout* (that redistributes power to cus-tomer champions), *capability* (by developing employees' skills) and *connection* (with partners).

Resilient organizations will also be more agile and able to make timely, effective and sustained changes to stay ahead of the competition in a fast-changing business context (Worley and Pillans 2015), or "(having) the ability to successfully manage uncertainty" (Teece et al. 2016, p. 8). Vecchiato (2015) applied a strategic foresight lens to propose that agile organizations outperform their rivals since they are better equipped to pursue first-mover advantages and build the skills to act on their learning, especially in turbulent environments. They are equipped with the necessary dynamic capabilities for efficiently and effectively redirecting their resources to higher-yielding activities. They are better able to innovate, adapt to turbulence and create change that delivers superior customer value (Teece et al. 2016).

## Strategic foresight and vigilance

Persuasive evidence of the performance gains resulting from superior foresight – a dynamic sensing capability – comes from a longitudinal study by Rohrbeck and Kum (2018). They assessed the future preparedness of 85 European multinationals in 2008, then waited eight years to measure the gain in market capitalization in 2015. This time lag was judged long enough to see tangible performance differences from strategic foresight. Their measure of the foresight capability was derived from a study of the peripheral vision of organizations (Day and Schoemaker 2004) incorporating outside-in indicators.

The foresight capability was measured relative to the need for vigilance, based on the complexity and volatility of the environment. Multiple measures were used to score each firm along these two dimensions; reasonable cutoffs were then used to place firms in one of four categories. This classification yielded 36 percent of firms deemed vigilant by the researchers in 2008, owing to their superior foresight capabilities in a turbulent environment. This group was 33 percent more profitable in 2015 (measured as earnings before interest, tax, depreciation, and amortization) than the rest of the firms. The vigilant firms also had a 75 percent gain in their market capitalization since 2008, whereas those deemed vulnerable gained only 38 percent over the same seven-year period.

## Innovation and firm performance

There have been enough studies of the effects of market and outside-in orientations on innovation and firm performance to populate two meta-analyses. The results are generally supportive of the hypothesized performance benefits, subject to qualifications owing to the usual difficulty of untangling the interdependencies of a firm's internal resources, capabilities and market position (Henderson and Mitchell 1997).

A meta-analysis of the effect of outside-in orientation (Saeed et al. 2015) was based on a database of 232 studies reported in 15 marketing and management journals. This study found that an inside-out orientation had a greater impact on innovation performance (number of new products, new product success rates, and pioneering activities) than did an outside-in orientation. However, an outside-in orientation had a stronger effect on firm performance measures (profitability, growth in sales and market share, and shareholder equity). Some of the differences between innovation and firm performance may be owing to the breadth, comparability, and quality of the latter measures.

A sharper picture of the relationship emerged from the meta-analysis by Kirca et al. (2005) of the performance consequences of a market orientation. This study had the advantage of a consistent usage across studies of the same specification of market orientation, as defined by Kohli and Jaworski (1990). Kirca et al. (2005) found a mean value of the expected effect on revenue performance of r = .32. They also found that a market orientation enhanced firm profits (r = .27), after accounting for the cost of implementing a market orientation, and the relationship was consistently stronger in the manufacturing versus the service sector. They posited that a market orientation may function more as a failure preventer in service companies and as a success inducer in manufacturing firms.

To buttress the findings on the overall relationship of market orientation and profitability there have also been investigations of the influence of outside-in marketing capabilities on firm performance (Vorhies et al. 2009). These capabilities represent the ability of a firm to sense market changes, engage with customers, and link with partners. These are also essential ingredients of a dynamic sensing capability. Both specialized (task-specific) and architectural (directing the coordination of specialized activities) marketing capabilities were strong and positive mediators of the relationship of the product-market strategy and cash flow performance.

## Summary of the performance effects

The weight of evidence about performance is strongly supportive of the gains from an outside-in orientation. This evidence further reveals that it is the interconnections of outside-in and inside-out approaches that also matter. This returns us to an initial premise of this book, that strategy formulation is an iterative learning process that yields superior results when begun from the outside in.

The purpose of this diagnosis was to identify the properties that distinguish organizations best able to successfully formulate and implement strategy from the outside in, and explain how and why this approach yields superior long-run performance.

The achievement of these purposes was a path-dependent process building on cumulative progress in the research domains of dynamic capabilities, market orientation, and design thinking. The basis of the outside-in approach is an iterative learning process starting with a wide-angle sensing of changes in the conditions in the ecosystem, including external stakeholders, present and potential rivals, and key influencers. For this strategy-making process to yield superior results, it must be conducted within a supportive organization with four properties, starting with the essential ingredient of leadership commitment to this decision-making priority and mental model. This leadership commitment is realized through the further properties of an empathetic orientation, catalyzed by collective curiosity, with a system-wide emphasis on developing superior foresight. The outcome is an organization with a strategy that is agile and resilient amid rising turbulence.

# 9    Preparing marketing for greater turbulence

Marketing is at the interface of the firm and its current and prospective markets, and is the organizational function that absorbs a large amount of the environmental turbulence. How will the activities, responsibilities, and design of the marketing organization evolve in the future? The answers to these questions will emerge from the interplay of the unique features of a firm's strategy, legacy, and market dynamics, with three driving forces: (1) the impact of digital technologies, (2) intensifying market turbulence, and (3) emerging organizational designs. The chief marketing/commercial/customer officer will be our lens to assess the impact of these driving forces on the practice of marketing. Through this lens we see why so many firms will have to reinvent their marketing organizations and become more outside-in in their approach to strategy.

When thinking about the future of marketing, five years is a long time. To appreciate what can happen in five years, think back to 2016–17: blockchains were mostly about crypto-currencies, and the rapid acceptance of social media platforms had glossed over the concerns about privacy and misinformation which are now emerging. The external shocks from the global pandemic of 2020–21 that revealed the fragility of global supply chains, were barely foreseen. We can be sure that five years from now there will be equally dramatic surprises. Yet there are some predictable changes – the consequences of the three driving forces – that are already at work, and that chief marketing officers (CMOs) and their C-suite partners can prepare for with confidence that they will be realized.

The forces of change are causes, as well as consequences, of the environmental turbulence coursing through all markets. This wider setting can be more fully appreciated by mapping the zones of uncertainty facing the firm in the future. Figure 9.1 is a map of these zones developed for a global business-to-business (B2B) manufacturing firm, with a lengthy and vulnerable supply chain. These and other sources of uncertainty may combine in unpredictable ways to increase turbulence. Leaders naturally wonder what else may be coming over the horizon. It is in the nature of uncertainty that it defies precise predictions about the likelihood, timing, and impact of future shocks. Answers to the questions of when, where, and how will be shrouded in doubt. Still, it is quite possible to explore the various zones of uncertainty and prepare in advance.

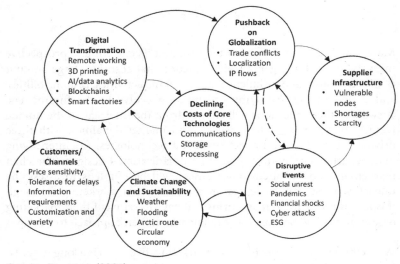

**Source:** Day et al. (2021).

**Figure 9.1**    Mapping zones of uncertainty

The most immediate impression from Figure 9.1 is the extent of the interactions among the seven zones. Our emphasis in this chapter is on those zones most directly contributing to digital and market turbulence. One message is that no single digital technology promotes digital turbulence. Instead, it is an effect of the simultaneous maturing of multiple core technologies, dramatic declines in their costs, new functionalities, and new platforms to put them to work. The unpredictability of these processes creates turbulence which is further accentuated by surprises from disruptive events, the looming threat of climate change, and impediments to further globalization.

## Digital turbulence

Marketing is one of the most technology-dependent functions in the firm. By 2018, CMOs were spending more on digital technologies than were chief information officers. Approaches for analyzing markets and interacting with customers that were at the cutting-edge a few years ago are fast becoming obsolete, and new approaches emerge regularly. The broad nature of these new approaches is widely known. What is less appreciated is how they are changing marketing practice.

*New ways of understanding and connecting with customers.* Next practice marketers are using customer analytics, predictive analytics, and customer experience mapping to deliver integrated experiences that are compelling, personalized, and consistent across all the points at which the firm touches their customers. They have many ways of connecting with these customers (video, Short Message Service or SMS, social media, websites, and mobile devices) as well as familiar direct mail, sponsorships, and traditional media. Some chief executive officers (CEOs) say that digital marketing investments are the most important commitments their firms can make because they reshape the firm's relationship with their customers. Also, these investments enable competitors to gain an advantage if the firm responds too slowly.

This burst of technology innovation is proving hard to manage effectively. In addition to established platforms for customer relationship management (CRM), content management, and marketing automation, there are many new platforms for social media management, content marketing and customer-facing engagement. Their impact is felt differently in different industries; banking is being transformed by mobility and blockchain-enabled payment systems, as well as the ability to personalize offers. Conversely, building products manufacturers serving only B2B markets will pay attention to CRM, salesforce control models, and social media.

*Advances in decision tools.* Fortunately, there is progress in methods for absorbing, interpreting, and acting on the avalanche of data being generated by fragmenting markets and the proliferation of digital media and channels for reaching customers (Wedel and Kannan 2016). Whereas marketers once had to exert significant effort to gain feedback from their customers; now they struggle to absorb the feedback from user-generated content and social media channels. In many markets we are close to being able to tailor the message and offer to each customer and prospect. The fuel is the plummeting cost of bandwidth, storage, and computing, and the consequence is that available data is doubling every 18 months.

There is an ever-widening gap between the ability of firms to comprehend and use the data and the growing amount of data they are receiving (Day 2011). Advances in digital technology will help narrow this gap, at least for those firms able to master the technology and build an organization capable of using expert systems and artificial intelligence approaches. Consider the potential of IBM's Watson, a cognitive technology that is a natural extension of what humans can do. Watson can read and understand natural language, which is important in analyzing the unstructured data that currently make up as much as 80 percent of data.

## Market turbulence

A story of one company's response to the disruption owing to the pandemic reveals why firms must build more agile organizations. When Medsys (disguised), a global life sciences firm, rethought their go-to-market strategy, as the uncertainty of the pandemic abated, they built on what they had learned during their adjustment. The Commercial Director was about to appoint a taskforce of sales leaders to plan the resumption of their direct sales model as soon as travel was possible. Instead, the leadership team called for a timeout to rethink their costly, traditional approach. Two internal teams were formed, each with a salesperson, a customer service manager, and a product specialist, to make virtual visits to large accounts. They were to listen to what their customers had experienced, to learn what they liked and disliked about all their suppliers, and how they saw the future. They learned that most customers were comfortable with the online contacts and enthusiastic about continuing with digital connections for their routine interactions.

Meanwhile, markets have become more turbulent and marketing has never been more complex. Leadership teams struggle to anticipate what may lie around the corner when:

- Digital platforms help new global players to emerge in unexpected ways. China now has a large lead in the ability to make mobile payments (roughly 50 times that of the US). In just 15 years, the number of Chinese firms in the Fortune Global 500 has increased more than 20 times.
- Market boundaries are blurring and dissolving. Financial technologies (fintech), are altering the nature of money itself, including how customers transact and secure loans. Big bets are being made by companies on blockchain technologies that enable cryptocurrencies for the decentralized electronic exchanges of value.
- The pace of change keeps accelerating. With the compression of time, the gap between the rate of change and the ability of traditional, hierarchical organizations to keep up is widening.

Why are some firms more adept at anticipating the opportunities and threats from digital and market turbulence, while others struggle to keep up? One answer is that the winners have developed superior vigilance capabilities they can routinely exercise through deeply embedded organizational processes (Day and Schoemaker 2019). Even though nearly every organization will be blindsided at some time in the next year, the vigilant firms are better prepared to respond. They know that the narrative "it is not going to happen to us" offers false comfort. To avoid the trap of complacency, leaders in vigilant firms keep the following three navigation principles in mind.

*Navigation principle 1: paying attention is a deliberate act.* Vigilant organizations carefully manage which of the bewildering array of external and internal issues they need to attend to, and which can be ignored. They know that attention is the scarcest of all organizational resources since it constrains the capacity to focus on, and respond to, pressing issues each day. To pay attention to everything is equivalent to paying attention to nothing. As Herbert Simon wrote in 1971 (p. 39), "[A] wealth of information creates a poverty of attention. More information is not always a good thing if it leads to blinkered thinking and analysis paralysis."

So, how should leaders allocate their organization's limited attention, including their own? Within vulnerable firms, leaders direct most of their attention inward toward current operations to meet short-term performance targets, using any scarce remaining time to react to unexpected events, unwelcome surprises, or internal political tensions of the moment. These leaders seldom have time left to reflect on the bigger picture and discuss what really matters in the future. Hence, their response to unexpected change tends to be weak, fragmented, and rushed.

*Navigation principle 2: adopt a new perspective on speed.* Once organizations have sensed an incipient change and are starting to understand what it could mean, the question becomes, what action to take? Amid digital and market turbulence, speed is an especially useful creed. First, delays usually increase the damage and narrow the opportunity range, if someone gets to them sooner. Second, seeing sooner gives more time to create strategic options to be exercised when the time is right – thus avoiding hasty, irreversible investments. Finally, there are well-documented benefits from moving first (Stalk 1990; Torbert 2004).

Just because the clock of business is whirring faster does not mean that leaders must operate in haste. Acting faster than rivals is about being ready for action when needed, and this starts with early detection and learning through probing questions and exploratory forays. Only after sufficient clarity has been achieved about key issues can leaders orchestrate better organizational preparedness in the form of multiple options and contingency plans. The aim of seeing sooner is to have more degrees of freedom later, when quick or bold actions are called for, without being boxed in by rivals' moves. Most managers prefer to act on their own terms rather than be forced to react to someone else's initiative.

*Navigation principle 3: vigilance capabilities foster agility.* Organizations at the bleeding edge of digital and market turbulence are moving from a comfortable and known risky environment (where decision outcomes can be specified and probabilities calculated) toward the deep uncertainty of unknown unknowns. Familiar and predictable environments can usually be navigated by "doing things right," and using ordinary capabilities for the proficient execution of current processes. To navigate deep uncertainty, in contrast, requires a more vigilant toolkit based on two dynamic capabilities: *sensing* change sooner than rivals and *seizing* opportunities more effectively.

Which dynamic sub-capabilities to emphasize depends on the situation. When there are many high-risk, capital-intensive opportunities to consider, such as those DuPont faced when exploring alternative energies that could leverage their biotechnology expertise, a mastery of the real-options analysis sub-capability is essential. However, when deploying digital technologies that are widely available and require smaller investments within tight time frames, leaders must emphasize different sub-capabilities. For example, when Novartis equipped its sales representatives with interactive digital devices so they could engage in consultative two-way dialogues with prescribing doctors, they needed to rely on a highly tuned vigilant learning sub-capability (Day and Schoemaker 2016). In these two examples, at least six multiple sub-capabilities were used, ranging from peripheral scanning and real options analysis, to organizational redesigns and culture changes. However, the relative weights given to each component varied by circumstance.

With the correct set of dynamic capabilities, an organization becomes agile when turbulence is high. Agility here means being able to move quickly and adroitly shift resources to higher-value activities sooner than rivals can. For example, agile strategies are activated when a scrum is formed to tackle an emerging opportunity or address a recent threat. A small team or scrum of three to nine people is quickly assembled with all the diverse skills needed to carry out the initiative. They function as self-managing teams, following a transparent process, using design thinking methods (Carlgren et al. 2016; Beckman 2020) to develop and test prototype solutions, and learn quickly. These features are the antithesis of cumbersome, top-down innovation processes with repetitive meetings, extensive documentation, and other impediments to progress.

## Implications for marketing organizations

A marketing organization has four reinforcing elements (the 4Cs). The first element is a firm's marketing *capabilities*, which are the complex bundles of firm-level skills and knowledge that guide marketing activities and the adaptation of a firm to marketplace changes. Second, by creating values, norms, and behaviors that facilitate a focus on the market, a market-oriented *culture* guides thinking and actions throughout the firm. Third, the marketing *configuration* comprises the organizational structures, metrics, and incentives/control systems that influence marketing activities. This configuration is the organizational setting within which marketing capabilities are exercised and culture is activated. Fourth, marketing leaders and employees are the (human) *capital* that creates, implements, and evaluates a firm's strategy. These four marketing organization elements should be reinforcing, as when a supportive culture attracts superior talent (Moorman and Day 2016).

Companies are being pulled by their strategies and pushed by digital turbulence and assertive customers to rethink their organizations. The objective is to enable the effective exercise of the dynamic marketing capabilities of: vigilant market learning (to see threats and opportunities sooner), adaptive experimentation and risk taking, and open marketing (Day 2011). In response, they are flattening (or delayering) to remove layers in the traditional closed hierarchy (Wulf 2012), and augmenting this structure with an open-network approach that shrinks the core of the organization while expanding the periphery. The emerging organization will have the following three features.

*Customer-centric structures.* Customer-centric structures – defined as a structural design where a firm's highest-level business units are aligned to distinct customer groups rather than to product groups – can serve as the means to building a fluid organization. A customer-centric structure generates "accountability for managing customer relationships," creates a shared, within-unit focus on customers and improves responsiveness to customer needs (Lee et al. 2015, p. 75). A customer-centric structure allows each business unit to quickly sense the shifts in the market and foster cross-functional activities, and enables employees to better navigate changing technologies and customer data (for example, social media marketing, discussions in online communities, and digital contents), and to act on the new information more effectively. By contrast, within a firm with product-based units, multiple units might target the same customers, creating confusion for customers and disrupting relationship-building efforts (Day 2006).

Aligning units to mirror customer groups also comes with a cost. To deliver offerings to customers as an integrated experience, the front-end and back-end offices need to converge to provide seamless customer solutions. This process requires a duplication of infrastructure and functions, so structural complexity arises and must be resolved through sophisticated internal coordination mechanisms. For example, Cisco Systems reverted from a customer-centric structure to a product-centric structure owing to the unbearable resource duplications and costs of: "the same or similar products [to] different customer segments" (Gulati 2009, p. 102). Yet, digital connectedness can lower the coordinating costs associated with a customer-centric structure; firms can find more efficient ways to combine and reconfigure their resources, allowing them to better navigate rapidly shifting technologies and customer voices.

*Structural granularity.* Structural granularity is the extent to which a firm divides itself into small structural units. While a customer-centric structure involves significant organizational changes in the structural archetype, which determines groupings and coordination of resources, structural granularity involves smaller-scale changes, such as additions, deletions, and new combinations of structural units. Disaggregating a firm into smaller structural units increases agility by allowing each unit to be closely engaged with target customers, improving employees' responsive to customers' changing needs. In addition, granular units can be more effective at launching smaller-scale experiments that can position the organization to seize fleeting opportunities while learning from these trials and errors. This type of structure empowers individuals and allows them to quickly identify any minuscule changes in the market (Blenko et al. 2010; Berlin et al. 2017).

Some of the agility benefits may be offset by sacrificing economies of scale, creating functional redundancies, and encouraging resource competition among units. Smaller units inherently provide customer-centricity benefits, but some customers still may need to interact with multiple units, which would require firms to institute additional customer-centric processes (for example, sales programs) that reduce the customer's communication burden (Kumar et al. 2008).

*Networked teams.* Networked teams – an interconnected cluster of project- or task-based teams whose activities last a short period of time – increase learning agility of employees by increasing flexibility of knowledge transfers, and fostering informal communication. A network structure might not have an organizational chart. It often consists of voluntary ad hoc groups but also can be designed as part of a formal structure. Network structures enhance cross-boundary (for example, customer-firm and cross-functional) knowledge sharing and cooperation, and improve innovation performance (Lee et al. 2015).

It is difficult to implement this form of structure in the organization as coordination imposes complexities, since firms can constantly change units' responsibilities; this often means more confusion within the firm. The key is to clarify accountability when employees work as a network of teams. Indeed, "degree of complexity of an organizational structure or form (e.g. tall vs. flat; matrix, virtual matrix, network form) impacts the nature, rate, and diffusion of different activities within an organization, such as information processing, knowledge sharing, routine replication, and capability development" (Felin et al. 2012, p. 1365). Perhaps block-chain technologies can reduce transaction costs so the organizational boundaries will become more fluid and porous; by reducing the costs of search in the firm and finding resources in a timelier manner. For example, ConsenSys, a venture production studio, used a blockchain technology to flatten the structure; works and contributions are codi-fied in smart contracts, and the structure functions as a hub-and-spoke arrangement where the technology provides supporting services.

## Bringing the future forward

The turbulence and uncertainty owing to the pandemic has also accel-erated trends in organization design that were already in motion. In the post-coronavirus future, leaders will have to find a balance between what worked before and what needs to be happen to succeed in the future. The following four trends are especially pertinent.

*Trend 1: the future of work.* Most executives were pleased with how well their organizations pivoted to working remotely. This also required organ-izations to rethink how they enabled, trained, and socialized employees. However, more than 70 percent of jobs cannot be performed entirely off site. Thus, the challenge will be to institutionalize what worked, become more decentralized, and depend less on top-down command-and-control decision making. The trend will continue toward agile teams that are allowed to make day-to-day decisions, while reserving the big-bet deci-sions to the leadership team. Routine decisions will be made much lower in the structure, to good effect.

*Trend 2: "more is not better".* This was in the title of Roger Martin's (2020) incisive book, with the prescient sub-title "Overcoming America's Obsession with Economic Efficiency." He shows that optimizing for profits can, intentionally or unintentionally, create brittle systems that are not versatile or sustainable. When the separate components of a system are individually optimized, the overall system becomes less resilient. This reality certainly impacted marketers who had to deal with supply-chain problems that interfered with their ability to meet commitments to customers. Their highly optimized and increasingly lengthy supply chains proved more fragile than expected. Reliance on a few, highly specialized suppliers with scale advantages, limited their degrees of freedom when they experienced unexpected shocks. These problems are being exacerbated by the political and social resistance to globalization (Day et al. 2021).

*Trend 3: evolving ecosystems.* As firms become more interconnected, unexpected partnerships are emerging. There is an incentive to form ecosystems through partnerships and joint ventures to expand capabilities. Inevitably these ecosystems will compete; this week's competitor may be next month's supplier, customer, partner, or all of these. Although the Apple and Samsung ecosystems compete fiercely in the mobile phone market, Apple also relies on Samsung for key components for its devices.

*Trend 4: The digital transformation of industries.* This transformation accelerated during the pandemic. The transition to remote work and virtual meetings is one of many profound changes. Another is "TeleXaas" or the rise of "everything" as a service that can be delivered online, and sometimes replacing traditional in-person experiences. These digital capabilities are the product of breathtaking advances in computer system performance, including processing, storing, and communicating. Artificial intelligence – which can learn from its environment and take autonomous action – has profound implications for marketing. Some provocative possibilities are described by Kumar (2021).

## The changing role of the C-suite

When people reach the C-suite, the skills and functional mastery that got them there matter less than their leadership skills and general business acumen (Groysberg et al. 2011). The chief information officer, chief technology officer, or CMO who thrives in the C-suite will be a team member who can lead without rank, with an organizational behind them that has earned the respect of the rest of the organization. The skills that are increasingly in favor in the C-suite are strong communications, a willingness to partner with other functions, and strategic thinking. Successful members of the C-suite will advise the CEO on key decisions and strategic choices, but also offer their own well-informed insights.

For marketing leaders to thrive and survive in a collaborative C-suite, they will have to adopt a general management mind-set and earn the respect of their peers with fact-based analyses. They will achieve the status of a trusted advisor to the CEO by:

- Being the acknowledged voice of the customer and consumer, and ensuring the strategy is built and executed from the outside in. That is, standing in the customer's shoes and viewing everything the firm does through the customer's eyes.
- Being the steward of the brand as a valuable asset, and rallying the entire organization to support and enhance the brand promise.
- Driving profitable organic growth, by continually searching for new ways to innovate new value for customers. They consider the full spectrum of possibilities for growth, instead of limiting themselves to the narrower possibilities of product innovation.
- Taking accountability for the returns on marketing investments.

They will gain further credibility by building a marketing organization that is fluid, agile, and informed by data and deep insights into the current and potential customers – and that is demonstrably superior to the rivals. This model of a CMO flourishes in business-to-consumer (B2C) firms with big global brands.

Within B2B companies, we are likely to find marketing leaders serving as *market advocates*. Their main roles are to be advocates for outside-in approaches, and to serve as a credible source of market insights (Fahey 2018). While their aspirations may be expansive, they are primarily coordinators and communicators, although they may have an increased influence as an integrator of digital strategies to enhance the customer experience. In other B2B companies this role is even more limited and even less influential. *Service resource marketers* also have sundry administrative responsibilities, such as monitoring compliance with brand or trademark guidelines. This model of a strictly supportive marketing function is found at science-based and high-technology firms, with strong research and development cultures, in which product managers have complete profit and loss responsibility. Marketing often plays a limited *sales support* role in smaller B2B firms that are reliant on intermediaries. In these firms, sales usually prevails in the battle over budget allocations (Kotler et al. 2006). The relative power of sales is strengthened further if the most powerful customers, such as Walmart, expect to be served by multifunctional teams coordinated by sales.

## Implications for marketing

Fluid organizations continuously scan for potential opportunities in markets, emerging white spaces, and changing customer needs. They win by seeing opportunities sooner than their rivals do. This will take an experimental mind-set, a willingness to learn quickly from mistakes, and the ability to identify, test, and deploy new business models. They will achieve this goal when the marketing leader acts on five priorities.

1. *Build superior marketing capabilities.* The CMO of the future must fulfill many roles and embrace sometimes competing, even contradictory, forces both within and outside the organization. Among the most challenging is the need to deliver business results immediately, while creating the business of tomorrow. Both are essential to a healthy business (and a successful CMO), but require very different marketing processes, skills, and capabilities.

Delivering in the short term requires more proven, predictable, and repeatable tools, skills and processes embodied in ordinary capabilities. It is more left than right brained. These marketing capabilities require developing and executing repeatable models, simplification, executional discipline, rigorous measurement, and decisive action. Convergence, focus and delivery, with a more short-term mind-set is required. The CMO who does not master these ordinary capabilities and build them in the organization probably will not get the chance to spend much time on the longer-term challenges and opportunities.

Creating the business of tomorrow is an equally critical and longer-term challenge. The CMOs who do not master these dynamic capabilities will also find themselves at risk. The dynamic capabilities needed to identify and prepare the organization to seize the future – finding new opportunities and addressing the challenge of changing consumer and competitive environments – are different from the ordinary today capabilities. These require divergence and adaptive market experimentation (versus codification and convergence), vigilant market learning guided by curiosity (versus conformance), and the open-ended creative skills of innovation and design thinking.

2. *Bring an outside-in perspective to the strategy dialogue.* The marketing leader has customarily been the "voice of the customer." The sources of their influence are well known (Feng et al. 2015). However, with a broadening mandate from the leadership team they can and should evolve to become the authority and advocate for starting the strategy dialogue from the outside in, and bringing deep insights about the demand-side ecosystem into strategic decisions. The credibility of these marketing leaders will depend on their mastery of customer insights, competitive strategies, and foresight capabilities.

Marketing leaders will also cultivate the organizational properties that are most conducive to the successful formulation of outside-in strategies: an empathetic orientation that is catalyzed by collective curiosity, and an emphasis on looking forward. They will achieve this by leading through their example – they genuinely live this perspective – and by role modeling to their functional organization. They are persistent champions of this approach, reminding everyone of success stories (or inside-out failures), and by using every occasion to educate others in what it means and how thinking from the outside in benefits the organization.

3. *Integrate digital technologies.* In a digital world, software is the vehicle for engaging prospects, current customers, and recapturing defectors. The choice of software and its configuration and deployment can dramatically affect how the firm is seen by customers. This means mastering a new set of capabilities, supporting them with investment spending, and interfacing with service providers, agencies, and research firms that have to be managed as partners.

In this changing digital space, the CMO and chief information officer (CIO) must collaborate closely. One way to manage this interface in a holistic fashion, to ensure that what is possible with technology inspires what is needed by marketing (and vice versa), is to engage a new type of hybrid executive: the chief marketing technologist (CMT) (Brinker and McLellan 2014). Their job is to serve as the connective tissue between marketing, information technology (IT) and external partners.

The CMT cannot achieve this digital integration on his or her own. Most companies are facing a crisis in finding the talented people who understand the fast-changing digital landscape. Everyone wants the same scarce set of skills to undertake data analytics, utilize knowledge-sharing technologies, and deploy social media methods. Marketers will have to work with human resource professionals to identify the skill sets needed in the future, and develop a continuous talent-spotting and recruitment process.

There is a generational transformation underway currently in marketing that is both a challenge and an opportunity. For most of the past, the future generation learned at the "knees of the elders," as experience and wisdom were the primary sources of knowledge, expertise, and ultimate success. With the digital technology-led transformation of strategies, it is the "future generation" who have the greater knowledge, understanding, and comfort with the new digital and social-marketing applications.

The fluid organization will recognize the value from obtaining the best from the digital marketers, and will neither be stuck in the past nor discard all the institutional knowledge and experience in jumping to a completely new model of marketing. The fundamentals of marketing strategy, customer value propositions, and consumer behavior have not been repealed. A fluid organization will study the changes, understand how the consumer interacts with the new marketing technologies, challenge old models and tactics, and experiment with new ones. They will figure out what works in the new digital environment for their business and customer, and evolve their models and practices.

4. *Tightening the alignment with sales.* Too often there is an adversarial Mars versus Venus coloration to the relationship of sales and marketing. It has historically been rooted in mutual incomprehension of the other's role, different time horizons, and divergent goals and incentives. Typically, the two functions occupied separate silos, and one function had more power than the other, depending on the industry.

The traditional lines between marketing and sales are blurring. Key account managers serving large, powerful customers are engaged in long-run marketing strategy and brand development activities. Meanwhile, the number of possible points of contact with customers and consumers has been increasing exponentially, with social media, interactivity, and mobility demanding closer coordination. Increasingly, CEOs are looking for a single point of contact with all market-facing activities, who can take responsibility for the value proposition, innovation, marketing, and sales across all platforms. Many companies have responded with a new combined role of chief commercial officer. This combined function ensures closer internal and external alignment, by using digital platforms to coordinate all marketing and sales activities – from customer-service representatives responding to complaints on blogs to systems for tracking sales calls and consumer search behavior.

5. *Taking accountability for the returns on marketing spending.* There is no foreseeable future where marketing will not have to demonstrate that it can earn acceptable returns on marketing investments. While there is, admittedly, a fair amount of craft (even art) in effective marketing, the discipline at its core exists to create value for the enterprise. The CMO who does not understand this, embrace it, and build a marketing culture and capability around value creation through the returns on its marketing investments, will not survive.

## Summary

For organizations to succeed when there is increasing turbulence and accelerating change, they will have to reinvent their marketing organization.

The CMO will succeed by first adopting the mind-set of the CEO, not the creative CMO. The marketing function exists to deliver increased enterprise value in the short, medium and long terms. It does so by owning both the numerator and denominator of the value equation – optimizing the ability of marketing to generate top-line growth (the numerator) and reducing the cost of delivering that growth (the denominator). The CMO needs to adopt this mind-set and create a marketing culture that fully embraces it. He or she needs to serve as the role model for the desired values and behavior, and embrace the core metrics and measurements – not avoid them.

# Appendix: what role for marketing leaders?

This question addresses the role of marketing, as a functional activity, in contributing to the formulation of a competitive strategy. Ideally, this strategy should be a product of the combined efforts of the entire leadership team, but on the outside-in aspects the leader of marketing should be the first among equals.

Strategy making should not be the sole purview of the chief executive officer (CEO), the chief operating officer (COO) and the board of directors. Effective strategies are most likely to emerge from the combined insights and thought processes of the senior leadership team (the C-suite or top management team). The most influential members of this team are strong communicators who collaborate with other functions and serve as credible advisors to the CEO on all key decisions. Far more than advocates for the interests of their function or group, they can overcome the natural tendency toward isolated organizational silos that concentrate on the immediate tasks.

Within this leadership team the relative influence of the marketing leader can be diagnosed with the 10-point checklist in Figure A.1. These require difficult judgments, and ideally there should be separate assessments by both the CEO or COO and the marketing leader. To some extent the influence is signaled by the title they are given. The chief marketing/commercial/customer officer will have more influence and is more likely to be a part of the leadership team, than someone with the title of Director of Marketing, Director of Marketing Communications, VP of Marketing Services, or Director of Sales Support.

(Check all that are applicable)

1. Trusted advisor to CEO: "Has a seat at the table" ☐
2. Catalyzer of top-line organic growth ☐
3. Partner in the vigilance process ☐
4. CEO's single point of contact for marketing and sales ☐
5. Point person for the total customer experience across all touch points ☐
6. Credible source of customer, market and competitive insights (represents "The voice of the customer") ☐
7. Integrator of social media initiatives and strategies ☐
8. Accountable for returns on all marketing investments ☐
9. Steward of the brand asset ☐
10. Chief communicator (responsible for advertising, public relations) ☐

Total
Score

**Figure A.1**   Diagnosing the influence of the marketing leader

## Assessing the leader of marketing

For our purposes it is sufficient to treat each of the indicators in Figure A.1 as equally important and simply add up the total number that are checked. This overall score is a "descriptive" picture that captures the role and influence of the marketing leader *as it is*, and not a "normative" judgment of what the role *should be*. If the CEO and the leadership team do not accept how limited the role is revealed to be, and want to adopt more of an outside-in approach to strategy, they should collectively decide to upgrade the role.

This advice is easier to offer than it is to follow. In many organizations there is a pervasive credibility gap faced by marketers. The problem as one observer noted is that "CEOs already see that their most important challenges are marketing ones – they just don't believe that marketers themselves can confront them" (Kumar 2004, p. 30). This underlines the importance of thinking clearly about both the actual and possible roles. These can be grouped into four categories:

1. *Top-line leader* (score of 7 to 10). In this role, marketing has a central strategic guidance function that directs all customer-facing activities and the vigilance capability, drives the organic growth agenda, and positions the organization to prepare for an uncertain future. It has ownership of the customer proposition. This marketing leader will be accountable for obtaining an acceptable return on all marketing investments, and may have direct oversight of the sales activities. This model of a chief marketing officer (CMO) flourishes in B2C companies with big global brands, such as Unilever or American Express.

2. *Market advocate* (score of 4 to 6). These marketing leaders differ from top-line leaders by having only a limited role in the broader strategy dialogue, and seldom have direct oversight of sales, strategy development, or product development. Their main roles are to be advocates for outside-in approaches, and serving as a credible source of market insights (Fahey 2018). While their aspirations may be expansive, they are primarily coordinators and communicators, although they may have an increased influence as an integrator of digital strategies to enhance the customer experience.

3. *Service resource* (score of 2 or 3). These leaders are closer to line managers, overseeing central marketing research activities while coordinating relationships with partners in social media outlets, advertising agencies and marketing research suppliers. Service resource marketers also have sundry administrative responsibilities, such as monitoring compliance with brand or trademark guidelines. This model of a strictly supportive marketing function is found at science-based and high-technology firms with strong R&D cultures, in which product managers have complete profit-and-loss responsibility.

4. *Sales support* (score of 1 or 2). This model is most prevalent in smaller B2B firms that are reliant on intermediaries. In these firms, sales usually wins the battle over budget allocations (Kotler et al. 2006). The relative power of sales is strengthened further if the most powerful customers, such as Walmart, expect to be served by large, multifunctional teams coordinated by sales.

## Summary

An organization's marketing leadership model falls into one of four categories, ranging from a lofty and influential "top-line leader" to a limited and supportive "sales support" manager. Regardless of their range of responsibilities and influence, they each have a central role in modeling what it means to adopt an outside-in approach to formulating a strategy.

# References

Aaker, D.A. (2020), *Owning Game-Changing Subcategories: Uncommon Growth in the Digital Age*, New York: Morgan James.

Adner, R. (2017), 'Ecosystem as structure: an actionable construct for strategy', *Journal of Management*, **43** (1), 39–58.

Adner, R. and Helfat, C.E. (2003), 'Corporate effects and dynamic managerial capabilities', *Strategic Management Journal*, **24** (10), 1011–25.

Almquist, E., Senior, J. and Bloch, N. (2016), 'The elements of value: measuring – and delivering – what consumers really want', *Harvard Business Review*, **94** (September), 47–53.

Anthony, S.D., Johnson, M.W., Sinfield, J. and Altman, E.J. (2008), *Innovator's Guide to Growth*, Boston, MA: Harvard Business Review Press.

Applewhite, W.R.E. and Frothingham, A. (2003), *And I Quote*, New York: Doubleday.

Barney, J. (1991), 'Firm resources and sustained competitive advantage', *Journal of Management*, **17** (1), 99–120.

Barney, J.B. and Clark, D.N. (2007), *Resource-Based Theory*, Oxford: Oxford University Press.

Bason, C. and Austin, R.D. (2019), 'The right way to lead design thinking', *Harvard Business Review* (March–April), 82–91.

Beckman, S.L. (2020), 'To frame or reframe: where might design thinking research go next?', *California Management Review*, **62** (2), 144–62.

Benner, M.J. and Tushman, M.L. (2003), 'Exploitation, exploration and process management: the productivity dilemma revisited', *Academy of Management Review*, **28** (2), 238–56.

Berlin, G., De Smet, A. and Sodini, M. (2017), 'Why agility is imperative for healthcare organizations', McKinsey & Company.

Birkinshaw, J. and Ansari, S. (2015), 'Understanding management models: going beyond "what" and "why" to "how" work gets done in organization', in N.J. Foss and T. Saebi (eds), *Business Model Innovation: The Organizational Dimensions*, Oxford: Oxford University Press, pp. 85–103.

Birkinshaw, J. and Ridderstrale, J. (2017), *Fast Forward: Make Your Company Fit for the Future*, Palo Alto, CA: Stanford University Press.

Blenko, M.W., Mankins, M.C. and Rogers, P. (2010), 'The decision-driven organization', *Harvard Business Review*, **88** (6), 54–62.

Boyd, E.D., Chandy, R.K. and Cunha, M. (2010), 'When do chief marketing officers affect firm value? A customer power explanation', *Journal of Marketing Research*, **47** (6), 1162–76.

Brandenberger, A. (2017), 'Where do great strategies really come from?', *Strategy Science*, **2** (December), 220–25.

Brandenburger, A.M. and Stuart, H. (1996), 'Value-based business strategy', *Journal of Economics and Management Strategy*, 5 (1), 5–24.

Brinker, S. and McClellan, L. (2014), 'The rise of the chief marketing technologist', *Harvard Business Review* (July–August).

Brodherson, M., Broitman, A., Cherok, J. and Robinson, K. (2021), 'A customer-centric approach to marketing in a privacy-first world', *McKinsey Quarterly* (May), 1–9.

Brown, T. (2008), 'Design thinking', *Harvard Business Review* (June), 23–8.

Business Roundtable (2019), 'Business Roundtable redefines the purpose of a corporation to promote an economy that serves all Americans', 19 August, Business Roundtable, Washington, DC.

Buzzell, R.D. and Gale B.T. (1987), *The PIMs Principles: Linking Strategy to Performance*, New York: Free Press.

Carlgren, L., Rauth, I. and Elmquist, M. (2016), 'Framing design thinking: the concept in idea and enactment', *Creativity and Innovation Management*, 25 (1), 38–57.

CB Insights (2020), '23 Lessons from Jeff Bezos' annual letter to shareholders', *Research Briefs*, 27 April.

Cendrowski, S. (2012), 'Nike's new marketing mojo', *Fortune*, 27 February, 81–8.

Challagalla, G., Murtha, B.R. and Jaworski, B. (2014), 'Marketing doctrine: a principles-based approach to guiding marketing decision-making in firms', *Journal of Marketing*, 78 (4), 4–20.

Chamberlain, A. and Zhao, D. (2019), 'The key to happy customers? Happy employees', *Harvard Business Review* (19 August).

Chesborough, H. (2003), *Open Innovation: The New Imperative for Creating and Profiting from Technology*, Boston, MA: Harvard Business School Press.

Christensen, C.M. (2016), *The Innovators Dilemma*, Boston, MA: Harvard Business Review Press.

Christensen, C.M., Hall, T., Dillon, K. and Duncan, D.S. (2016a), 'Know your customer's jobs to be to be done', *Harvard Business Review* (September), 54–62.

Christensen, C.M., Hall, T., Dillon, K. and Duncan, D.S. (2016b), *Competing Against Luck: The Story of Innovation and Customer Choice*, New York: Harper Collins.

Collis, D.J. and Montgomery, C. (1995), 'Competing on resources: strategy in the 1990s', *Harvard Business Review*, 73 (July–August), 118–28.

Colvin, G. (2020), 'The simple metric that's taking over big business', *Fortune* (June–July), 112–17.

D'Aveni, R. (1994), *Hypercompetition: Managing the Dynamics of Strategic Maneuvering*, New York: Free Press.

Dawar, N. and Bendle, N. (2018), 'Marketing in an age of Alexa', *Harvard Business Review* (May–June), 80–86.

Day, G.S. (1992), 'Marketing's contribution to the strategy dialogue', *Journal of the Academy of Marketing Science*, 20 (4), 323–9.

Day, G.S. (1999), 'Misconceptions about market orientation', *Journal of Marketing-Focused Management*, 4 (June), 5–16.

Day, G.S. (2006), 'Aligning the organization with the market', *MIT Sloan Management Review*, 48 (1), 41–9.

Day, G.S. (2011), 'Closing the marketing capabilities gap', *Journal of Marketing*, **75** (4), 183–95.

Day, G.S. (2020), 'The dynamics of customer value propositions: an outside-in perspective', *Industrial Marketing Management*, **87** (May), 316–19.

Day, G.S. and Moorman, C. (2010), *Strategy from the Outside In: Profiting from Customer Value*, New York: McGraw-Hill.

Day, G.S. and Schoemaker, P.J.H. (2004), 'Peripheral vision: sensing and acting on weak signals', *Long Range Planning*, **37** (2), 117–21.

Day, G.S. and Schoemaker, P.J.H. (2008), 'Are you a vigilant leader?', *MIT Sloan Management Review*, **40** (Spring), 43–51.

Day, G.S. and Schoemaker, P.J.H. (2016), 'Adapting to fast-changing markets and technologies', *California Management Review*, **58** (4), 59–77.

Day, G.S. and Schoemaker, P.J.H. (2019), *See Sooner, Act Faster: How Vigilant Leaders Thrive in an Era of Digital Disruption*, Boston, MA: MIT Press.

Day, G.S. and Schoemaker, P.J.H. (2021), 'Navigating digital turbulence', *Management and Business Review* (Winter).

Day, G.S., Schoemaker, P.J.H. and Todd, S. (2021), 'Is your supply chain ready for what's next?', *Supply Chain Management Review* (March–April), 18–23.

Day, G.S. and Shea, G. (2020), 'Changing the work of innovation', *California Management Review*, **63** (1), 41–60.

Dong, A., Garburo, M. and Lovallo, D. (2016), 'Generative sensing: a design perspective on the micro-foundations of sensing capabilities', *California Management Review*, **58** (4), 97–117.

Drucker, P.F. (1954), *The Practice of Management*, New York: Harper & Brothers.

Drucker, P.F. (1985), *Innovation and Entrepreneurship*, New York: Harper and Row.

Drucker, P.F. (1994), 'The theory of the business', *Harvard Business Review* (September–October), 95–104.

Du, R.Y., Netzer, O., Schweidel, D.A. and Mitra, D. (2021), 'Capturing marketing information to fuel growth', *Journal of Marketing*, **85** (1), 163–83.

Dyer, J. and Gregersen, H. (2017), 'How does Amazon stay at day one?', *Forbes*, 8 August, 1–16.

Emery, F.E. and Trist, E.L. (1965), 'The causal texture of organizational environments', *Human Relations*, **18** (1), 21–32.

Fahey, L. (2018), *The Insight Discipline: Crafting New Marketplace Understanding that Makes a Difference*, Chicago, IL: American Marketing Association.

Fahey, L. and Randall, R.M. (eds) (1998), *Learning from the Future: Competitive Foresight Scenarios*, New York: John Wiley & Sons.

Fehrer, J.A. (2020), 'Rethinking marketing: back to purpose', *AMS Review*, **10** (3), 179–84.

Felin, T., Foss, N.J., Heimeriks, K.H. and Madsen, T.L. (2012), 'Microfoundations of routines and capabilities: individuals, processes, and structure', *Journal of Management Studies*, **49** (8), 1351–74.

Feng, H., Morgan, N.A. and Rego, L.L. (2015), 'Marketing department power and firm performance', *Journal of Marketing*, **79** (September), 1–20.

Flint, J. (1997), 'Company of the year', *Forbes*, 13 January, 84.

Freedman, L. (2013), *Strategy: A History*, Oxford: Oxford University Press.

Friedman, M. (1970), 'The social responsibility of business is to increase its profits', *The New York Times Magazine*, 13 September.

Frishammar, J. and Parida, V. (2019), 'Circular business model transformation: a roadmap for incumbent firms', *California Management Review*, **61** (2), 5–29.

Gaddis, J.L. (2018), *On Grand Strategy*, New York: Penguin.

Gallino, S. and Rooderkerk, R. (2020), 'New product development in an omnichannel world', *California Management Review*, **63** (1), 81–98.

Gino, F. (2018), 'The business case for curiosity', *Harvard Business Review* (September–October), 48–57.

Girotra, K. and Netessine, S. (2014), 'Four paths to business model innovation', *Harvard Business Review* (July–August), 97–103.

Golder, P. and Tellis, G.J. (2002), *Will and Vision: How Latecomers Grow to Dominate Markets*, New York: McGraw-Hill.

Govindarajan, V. and Trimble, C. (2005), *10 Rules for Strategic Innovators: From Idea to Execution*, Boston, MA: Harvard Business School Press.

Govindarajan, V. and Trimble, C. (2012), *Reverse Innovation: Create Far from Home, Win Everywhere*, Boston, MA: Harvard Business School Press.

Groysberg, B., Kelly, K. and MacDonald, B. (2011), 'The new path to the C-suite', *Harvard Business Review*, **89** (March), 60–68.

Gulati, R. (2009), *Reorganize for Resilience: Putting Customers at the Center of Your Business*, Boston, MA: Harvard Business Press.

Harreld, J.B., O'Reilly, C.A. and Tushman, M. (2007), 'Dynamic capabilities at IBM: driving strategy into action', *California Management Review*, **49** (4), 21–43.

Henderson, R. and Mitchell, W. (1997), 'The interactions of organizational and competitive influences on strategy and performance', *Strategic Management Journal*, **18** (Summer), 5–15.

Hill, T. and Westbrook, R. (1997), 'SWOT analysis: it's time for a recall', *Long Range Planning*, **30** (11), 46–52.

Homburg, C. and Pflesser, C. (2000), 'A multiple-layer model of market-oriented organizational culture: measurement issues and performance outcomes', *Journal of Marketing Research*, **37** (4), 449–62.

Homburg, C., Theel, M. and Hohenberg, S. (2020), 'Marketing excellence: nature, measurement and investor valuations', *Journal of Marketing*, **84** (4), 1–22.

Humphreys, A. and Carpenter, G.S. (2018), 'Status games: market driving through social influence in the US wine industry', *Journal of Marketing*, **82** (5), 141–59.

Humphreys, A. and Carpenter, G.S. (2019), 'Should you ignore what your customers want? The great winemakers do', *Kellogg Insight*, 1 February.

Huston, L. and Sakkab, N. (2006), 'Connect and develop: inside Procter & Gamble's new model for innovation', *Harvard Business Review* (March), 58–66.

Isaacson, W. (2011), *Steve Jobs*, New York: Simon & Schuster.

Jaworski, B.J. and Kohli, A.K. (1993), 'Market orientation: antecedents and consequences', *Journal of Marketing*, **57** (3), 53–70.

Kahneman, D. (2011), *Thinking Fast and Slow*, New York: Farrar, Straus and Giroux.

Kalbach, J. (2021), *Mapping Experiences: A Complete Guide to Customer Alignment through Journeys, Blueprints, and Diagrams*, 2nd edn, Sebastopol, CA: O'Reilly Media.

Keeley, L., Pikkel, R., Quinn, B. and Walters, H. (2013), *Ten Types of Innovation: The Discipline of Building Breakthrough*, Hoboken, NJ: John Wiley & Sons.

Kets de Vries, M. (2016), 'Why empathy makes for stronger organizations', *Knowledge.insead.edu*, Leadership and Organisations blog, 25 July, accessed 6 January 2022 at https://knowledge.insead.edu/blog/insead-blog/why-empathy-makes-for-stronger-organisations-4815.

Key, T.M., Clark, T., Ferrell, O.C., Stewart, D.W. and Pitt, L. (2020), 'Marketing's theoretical and conceptual value proposition: opportunities to address marketing's influence', *AMS Review*, **10** (December), 151–67.

Kim, E.Y., Beckman, S.L. and Agogino, A. (2018), 'Design road mapping in an uncertain world: implementing a customer experience – focused strategy', *California Management Review*, **61** (1), 43–70.

Kim, W.C. and Mauborgne, R.A. (2014), *Blue Ocean Strategy Expanded Edition: How to Create Uncontested Market Space and Make the Competition Irrelevant*, Boston, MA: Harvard Business School Press.

Kirca, A.H., Jayachandran, S. and Bearden, W.O. (2005), 'Market orientation: a meta-analytic review and assessment of its antecedents and impact on performance', *Journal of Marketing*, **69** (April), 24–41.

Knight, E., Daymond, J. and Paroutis, S. (2020), 'Design-led strategy: how to bring design thinking into the art of strategic management', *California Management Review*, **62** (2), 30–52.

Kogut, B. and Zander, U. (1992), 'Knowledge of the firm: combinative capabilities and the replications of technology', *Organization Science*, **3** (3), 383–97.

Kohli, A.K. and Jaworski, B.J. (1990), 'Market orientation: the construct, research propositions, and managerial implications', *Journal of Marketing*, **54** (April), 1–18.

Kotler, P., Rackham, N. and Krishnaswamy, S. (2006), 'Ending the war between sales and marketing', *Harvard Business Review* (July–August), 68–78.

Kozlenkova, I.V., Samaha, S.A. and Palmatier, R.W. (2013), 'Resource-based theory in marketing', *Journal of the Academy of Marketing Science*, **42** (January), 1–21.

Krueger, A.O. (2020), *International Trade: What Everyone Needs to Know*, Oxford: Oxford University Press.

Kumar, N. (2004), *Marketing as Strategy: Understanding the CEO's Agenda for Driving Growth and Innovation*, Boston, MA: Harvard Business School Press.

Kumar, V. (2013), *101 Design Methods: A Structured Approach for Driving Innovation in Your Organization*, Hoboken, NJ: John Wiley & Sons.

Kumar, V. (2021), *Intelligent Marketing: Employing New-Age Technologies*, New Delhi: Sage Publications.

Kumar, V., Venkatesan, R. and Reinartz, W. (2008), 'Performance implications of adopting a customer-focused sales campaign', *Journal of Marketing*, **72** (5), 50–68.

Lafley, A.G. and Martin, R.L. (2013), *Playing to Win: How Strategy Really Works*, Boston, MA: Harvard Business School Press.

Lee, J.Y., Kozlenkova, I. and Palmatier, R. (2015), 'Structural marketing: using organizational structure to achieve marketing objectives', *Journal of the Academy of Marketing Science*, **43** (1), 73–99.

Leinwand, P. and Mainardi, C. (2013), 'Beyond functions', *Strategy & Leadership*, **70** (Spring), 58–63.

Levitt, T. (1960), 'Marketing myopia', *Harvard Business Review*, **38** (July–August), 24–47.

Lovallo, D. and Kahneman, D. (2003), 'Delusions of success: how optimism undermines executive decisions', *Harvard Business Review* (July–August).

Makadok, R. (2001), 'Toward a synthesis of the resource-based and dynamic capability views of rent creation', *Strategic Management Journal*, **22** (5), 387–402.

March, J.G. (1991), 'Exploration and exploitation in organizational learning', *Organization Science*, **2** (1), 71–87.

Martin, R. (2009a), *The Design of Business: Why Design Thinking Is the Next Competitive Advantage*, Boston, MA: Harvard Business School Press.

Martin, R. (2020), *When More Is Not Better: Overcoming America's Obsession with Economic Efficiency*, Boston, MA: Harvard Business School Press.

Martin, R.L. (2009b), *The Opposable Mind: Winning through Integrative Thinking*, Boston, MA: Harvard Business School Press.

McGrath, R.G. (2013), *The End of Competitive Advantage: How to Keep Your Strategy Moving as Fast as Your Business*, Cambridge, MA: Harvard Business Review Press.

McGrath, R.G. and MacMillan, I.C. (2005), *Market Busters: 40 Strategic Moves that Drive Exceptional Business Growth*, Boston, MA: Harvard Business School Press.

Meehan, S. (2017), 'Ryanair strategic positioning (A) July 2013' and 'Ryanair strategic positioning (B): always getting better', cases IMD-7-1872 and IMD-7-1873, Institute for Management Development, Lausanne.

Micheli, P., Wilner, S.J.S., Bhatti, S., Mura, M. and Beverland, M.B. (2019), 'Doing design thinking', *Journal of Product Innovation Management*, **36** (2), 124–48.

Mintzberg, H. (1990), 'The design school: reconsidering the basic premises of strategic management', *Strategic Management Journal*, **11** (3), 171–95.

Mintzberg, H. (1994), *The Rise and Fall of Strategic Planning*, New York: Free Press.

Mitchell, V.-W. (1999), 'Consumer perceived risk: conceptualisations and models', *European Journal of Marketing*, **33** (1/2), 163–95.

Moore, G.A. (2005), *Dealing with Darwin*, New York: Portfolio.

Moorman, C. and Day, G.S. (2016), 'Organizing for marketing excellence', *Journal of Marketing*, **80** (4), 6–35.

Morgan, N.A., Voorhies, D. and Mason, C. (2009), 'Market orientation, marketing capabilities and firm performance', *Strategic Management Journal*, **30** (8), 909–20.

Morgan, N.A., Whitler, K.A., Feng, H. and Chari, S. (2019), 'Research in marketing strategy', *Journal of the Academy of Marketing Science*, **47** (January), 4–29.

Narayan, V.K., Zane, L.J. and Kammerer, B. (2011), 'The cognitive perspective in strategy: an integrative view', *Journal of Management*, **37** (1), 305–51.

Narver, J.C. and Slater, S.F. (1990), 'The effect of a market orientation on business profitability', *Journal of Marketing*, **54** (4), 20–35.

O'Reilly, C.O. and Binns, A.J.M. (2019), 'The three stages of disruptive innovation: idea generation, incubation and scaling', *California Management Review*, **61** (3), 49–71.

Oberholzer-Gee, F. (2020), *Better, Simpler Strategy: A Value-Based Guide*, Boston, MA: Harvard Business School Press.

Ocasio, W. (1997), 'Towards an attention-based view of the firm', *Strategic Management Journal*, **18** (Summer Special Issue), 187–206.

Osterwalder, A. and Pigneur, Y. (2010), *Business Model Generation: A Handbook for Visionaries, Game Changers, and Challengers*, Hoboken, NJ: John Wiley & Sons.

Osterwalder, A., Pigneur, Y., Bernarda, G., Smith, A. and Panadakos, T. (2014), *Value Proposition Design: How to Create Products and Services Customers Want*, Hoboken, NJ: John Wiley & Sons.

Palmatier, R.W, Moorman, C. and Lee, J.Y. (2019), *Handbook on Customer Centricity: Strategies for Building a Customer-centric Organization*, Cheltenham, UK and Northampton, MA, USA: Edward Elgar.

Patnaik, D. (2009), *Wired to Care: How Companies Prosper When They Create Widespread Empathy*, New York: FT Press.

Pavlou, P.A. and Sawry, E.L. (2011), 'Understanding the elusive black box of dynamic capabilities', *Organization Science*, **42** (February), 239–72.

Payne, A., Frow, P. and Eggert, A. (2017), 'The customer value proposition: evolution, development and application in marketing', *Journal of the Academy of Marketing Science*, **45** (July), 467–89.

Payne, A., Frow, P., Steinhoff, L. and Eggert, A. (2020), 'Toward a comprehensive framework of value proposition development: from strategy to implementation', *Industrial Marketing Management*, **27** (May), 244–55.

Pederson, T. and Sorrn-Friese, H. (2015), 'A business model innovation by a late mover: containerization in Maersk Line', in N.J. Foss and T. Saebi (eds), *Business Model Innovation: The Organizational Dimension*, Oxford: Oxford University Press, pp. 217–39.

Pisano, G. (2015), 'You need an innovation strategy', *Harvard Business Review* (June), 44–54.

Porter, M. (1996), 'What is strategy?', *Harvard Business Review*, **74** (6), 61–78.

Porter, M. and Siggelkow, N. (2008), 'Contextuality within activity systems and sustainability of competitive advantage', *Academy of Management Perspective*, **22** (2), 34–56.

Porter, M.E. (1980), *Competitive Strategy: Techniques for Analyzing Industries and Competitors*, New York: Free Press.

Porter, M.E. (1991), 'Towards a dynamic theory of strategy', *Strategic Management Journal*, **12** (Winter), special issue, 95–117.

Prahalad, C.K. (1995), 'Weak signals versus strong paradigms', *Journal of Marketing Research*, **32** (August), iii–vi.

Prahalad, C.K. and Hamel, G. (1990), 'The core competence of the corporation', *Harvard Business* Review, **68** (May–June), 79–91.

Ramirez, R. and Selsky, J.W. (2016), 'Strategic planning in turbulent environments: social ecology approach to scenarios', *Long Range Planning*, **49** (1), 90–102.

Reibstein, D.J., Day, G.S. and Wind, Y. (2009), 'Is marketing academia losing its way?', *Journal of Marketing*, **73** (July), 1–3.

Roberts, J.H. and Lattin, J.M. (1991) 'Development and testing of a model of consideration set compositions', *Journal of Marketing Research*, **28** (November), 429–40.

Rogers, M., Chesbrough, H., Heaton, S. and Teece, D.J. (2019), 'Strategic management of open innovation: a dynamic capabilities perspective', *California Management Review*, **62** (1), 77–94.

Rohrbeck, R. and Kum, M.E. (2018), 'Corporate foresight and its impact on firm performance: a longitudinal analysis', *Technological Forecasting and Social Change*, **129** (April), 105–16.

Rumelt, R.P. (2011), *Good Strategy/Bad Strategy: The Difference and Why It Matters*, New York: Crown Business.

Rumelt, R.P., Schendel, D.E. and Teece, D.J. (1994), *Fundamental Issues in Strategy: A Research Agenda*, Boston, MA: Harvard Business School Press.

Rust, R.T. (2020), 'The future of marketing', *International Journal of Research in Marketing*, **37** (1), 15–26.

Saeed, S., Yousafza, S., Paladino, A. and De Luca, L.M. (2015), 'Inside-out and inside-out orientations: a meta-analysis of orientation's effects on innovation and firm performance', *Industrial Marketing Management*, **47** (May), 121–33.

Satell, G. (2017), 'The 4 types of innovation and the problems they solve', *Harvard Business Review* (June 21).

Sawhney, M., Wolcott, R.C. and Arronz, I. (2006), 'The 12 different ways for companies to innovate', *MIT Sloan Management Review*, **47** (3), 75–81.

Schoemaker, P.J.H. and Day, G.S. (2020), 'Determinants of organizational vigilance', *Futures and Forecast Science*, **2** (1), e24.

Schultz, H. and Yang, D.J. (1997), *Pour Your Heart into It: How Starbucks Built a Company One Cup at a Time*, New York: Hyperion.

Senge, P. (2006), *The Fifth Discipline: The Art and Practice of the Learning Organization*, revd edn, New York: Doubleday.

Simon, H.A. (1971), 'Designing organizations for an information rich world', in M. Greenberger (ed.), *Computers, Communication and the Public Interest*, Baltimore, MD: Johns Hopkins Press, pp. 37–72.

Stalk, G. (1990), *Competing Against Time: How Time-Based Competition Is Reshaping Global Markets*, New York: Simon & Schuster.

Teece, D.J. (2007), 'Explicating dynamic capabilities: the nature and micro-foundations of (sustainable) enterprise performance', *Strategic Management Journal*, **28** (13), 1319–50.

Teece, D.J. (2009), *Dynamic Capabilities and Strategic Management*, Oxford: Oxford University Press.

Teece, D.J. (2018), 'Business models and dynamic capabilities', *Long Range Planning*, **51** (February), 40–49.

Teece, D.J., Perteraf, M. and Leih, S. (2016), 'Dynamic capabilities and organizational agility: risk, uncertainty and strategy in the innovation economy', *California Management Review*, **58** (4), 13–35.

Tetlock, P.E. (2005), *Expert Political Judgment: How Good Is It? How Can We Know?*, Princeton, NJ: Princeton University Press.

Torbert, W.P. (2004), *Action Inquiry: The Secret of Timely and Transforming Leadership*, San Francisco, CA: Berrett-Koehler.

Treacy, M. and Wiersema, T. (1997), *The Discipline of Market Leaders*, New York: Basic Books.

Tuli, K.R., Kohli, A.K. and Bharadwaj, S.G. (2007), 'Rethinking customer solutions: from product bundles to relational processes', *Journal of Marketing*, 71 (3), 1–17.

Unger, D. (2018), 'Strategy in three dimensions', *Strategy + Business* (May), 38–45.

Urban, G.L. and von Hippel, E. (1986), 'Lead user analyses for the development of new industrial products', *Management Science*, 34 (5), 569–82.

Van Den Driest, F., Sthanvnathan, S. and Wood, K. (2016), 'Building an insights engine', *Harvard Business Review* (September), 64–74.

Varadarayan, R. (2010), 'Strategic marketing and marketing strategy: domain, definition, fundamental issues and foundational premises', *Journal of the Academy of Marketing Science*, 38 (2), 119–40.

Vargo, S.L. and Lusch, R.F. (2004), 'Evolving to a new dominant logic for marketing', *Journal of Marketing*, 68 (1), 1–17.

Vargo, S.L. and Lusch, R.F. (2017), 'Service-dominant logic 2025', *International Journal of Research in Marketing*, 34 (1), 46–67.

Vecchiato, R. (2015), 'Creating value through foresight: first mover advantages and strategic agility', *Technological Forecasting and Social Change*, 101 (September), 25–36.

Vorhies, D.W., Morgan, R.E. and Autry, C.W. (2009), 'Product-market strategy and the marketing capabilities of the firm: impact on market effectiveness and cash flow performance', *Strategic Management Journal*, 30 (December), 1310–34.

Webster, F.E. Jr (1992), 'The changing role of marketing in the corporation', *Journal of Marketing*, 56 (October), 1–17.

Webster, F.E. Jr (2002), *Market-Driven Management: How to Define, Develop and Deliver Customer Value*, 2nd edn, Hoboken, NJ: John Wiley & Sons.

Wedel, M. and Kannan, P.K. (2016), 'Marketing analytics for data-rich environments', *Journal of Marketing*, 80 (November), 97–121.

Wierenga, B. (2020), 'The study of important issues in an evolving field', *International Journal of Research in Marketing*, 38 (1), 18–28.

Wind, Y. (2008), 'A plan to reinvent the marketing we need today', *MIT Sloan Management Review* (Summer), 21–8.

Wirtz, B.W., Pistoia, A., Ulrich, S. and Gottel, V. (2016), 'Business models: origin, development and future research perspectives', *Long Range Planning*, 49 (1), 36–54.

Worley, C. and Pilans, G. (2015), 'Organisation agility', November, Corporate Research Forum, London.

Worm, S., Bharadwaj, S.G., Ulaga, W. and Reinartz, W.J. (2017), 'When and why do customer solutions pay off in business markets?', *Journal of the Academy of Marketing Science*, 45 (4), 490–512.

Wulf, J. (2012), 'The flattened firm: not as advertised', *California Management Review*, 55 (1), 5–23.

Young, I. (2015), *Practical Empathy: For Collaboration and Creativity in Your Work*, New York: Rosenfeld Media.

Zeithaml, V.A. (2000), 'Service quality profitability and the economic worth of customers: what we know and what we need to learn', *Journal of the Academy of Marketing Science*, **28** (1), 67–85.

Zeithaml, V.A., Jaworski, B.J., Kohli, A.K., Tuli, K.R., Vlaga, W. and Zaltman, G. (2019), 'A theories-in-use approach to building marketing theory', *Journal of Marketing*, **84** (November), 32–51.

Zenko, M. (2015), *Red Team: How to Succeed by Thinking Like the Enemy*, New York: Basic Books.

Zhang, X. and Yu, X. (2020), 'The impact of perceived risk on consumer's cross-platform buying behavior', *Frontiers in Psychology*, **11**, 592246.

Zott, C. and Amit, R. (2007), 'Business model design and the performance of entrepreneurial firms', *Organization Science*, **18** (2), 181–99.

Zott, C. and Amit, R. (2009), 'Business model design: an activity system perspective', *Long Range Planning*, **42** (2–3), 216–26.

# Index